MACMILLAN MODERN NOVELISTS

General Editor: Norman Page

MACMILLAN MODERN NOVELISTS

Published titles

E. M. FORSTER   Norman Page
WILLIAM GOLDING   James Gindin
MARCEL PROUST   Philip Thody
SIX WOMEN NOVELISTS   Merryn Williams
JOHN UPDIKE   Judie Newman
H. G. WELLS   Michael Draper

Forthcoming titles

ALBERT CAMUS   Philip Thody
JOSEPH CONRAD   Owen Knowles
FYODOR DOSTOEVSKI   Peter Conradi
WILLIAM FAULKNER   David Dowling
F. SCOTT FITZGERALD   John S. Whitley
GUSTAVE FLAUBERT   David Roe
JOHN FOWLES   Simon Gatrell
GRAHAM GREENE   Neil McEwan
HENRY JAMES   Alan Bellringer
JAMES JOYCE   Richard Brown
D. H. LAWRENCE   G. M. Hyde
DORIS LESSING   Ruth Whittaker
MALCOLM LOWRY   Tony Bareham
GEORGE ORWELL   Valerie Meyers
BARBARA PYM   Michael Cotsell
MURIEL SPARK   Norman Page
GERTRUDE STEIN   Shirley Neuman
EVELYN WAUGH   Jacqueline McDonnell
VIRGINIA WOOLF   Edward Bishop

MACMILLAN MODERN NOVELISTS
WILLIAM GOLDING

James Gindin

MACMILLAN

First published 1988

Published by
Higher and Further Education Division
MACMILLAN PUBLISHERS LTD
Houndmills, Basingstoke, Hampshire RG21 2XS
and London
Companies and representatives
throughout the world

Typeset by Wessex Typesetters
(Division of The Eastern Press Ltd)
Frome, Somerset

Printed in Hong King

British Library Cataloguing in Publication Data
Gindin, James
William Golding.—(Macmillan modern
novelists)
1. Golding, William—Criticism and
interpretation
I. Title
823'.914   PR6013.O35Z/
ISBN 0–333–40681–8
ISBN 0–333–40682–6 Pbk

Contents

Acknowledgments

The author and publishers wish to thank Faber and Faber Ltd for permission to reprint extracts from *The Hot Gates, The Spire, The Inheritors, Free Fall, Pincher Martin, The Pyramid, The Scorpion God, Lord of the Flies, Brass Butterfly, An Egyptian Journal, Darkness Visible, Rites of Passage, The Paper Men* and *The Moving Target*, all by William Golding.

Every effort has been made to trace all the copyright holders but if any have been inadvertently overlooked the publishers will be pleased to make the necessary arrangement at the first opportunity.

General Editor's Preface

The death of the novel has often been announced, and part of the secret of its obstinate vitality must be its capacity for growth, adaptation, self-renewal and even self-transformation: like some vigorous organism in a speeded-up Darwinian ecosystem, it adapts itself quickly to a changing world. War and revolution, economic crisis and social change, radically new ideologies such as Marxism and Freudianism, have made this century unprecedented in human history in the speed and extent of change, but the novel has shown an extraordinary capacity to find new forms and techniques and to accommodate new ideas and conceptions of human nature and human experience, and even to take up new positions on the nature of fiction itself.

In the generations immediately preceding and following 1914, the novel underwent a radical redefinition of its nature and possibilities. The present series of monographs is devoted to the novelists who created the modern novel and to those who, in their turn, either continued and extended, or reacted against and rejected, the traditions established during that period of intense exploration and experiment. It includes a number of those who lived and wrote in the nineteenth century but whose innovative contribution to the art of fiction makes it impossible to ignore them in any account of the origins of the modern novel; it also includes the so-called 'modernists' and those who in the mid and later twentieth century have emerged as outstanding practitioners of this genre. The scope is, inevitably, international; not only, in the migratory and exile-haunted world of our century, do writers refuse to heed national frontiers – 'English' literature lays claims to Conrad the Pole, Henry James the American, and Joyce the Irishman – but geniuses such as Flaubert, Dostoevski and Kafka have had an influence on the fiction of many nations.

Each volume in the series is intended to provide an introduction to the fiction of the writer concerned, both for those approaching him or her for the first time and for those who are already familiar with some parts of the achievement in question and now wish to place it in the context of the total *oeuvre*. Although essential information relating to the writer's life and times is given, usually in an opening chapter, the approach is primarily critical and the emphasis is not upon 'background' or generalisations but upon close examination of important texts. Where an author is notably prolific, major texts have been selected for detailed attention but an attempt has also been made to convey, more summarily, a sense of the nature and quality of the author's work as a whole. Those who want to read further will find suggestions in the select bibliography included in each volume. Many novelists are, of course, not only novelists but also poets, essayists, biographers, dramatists, travel writers and so forth; many have practised shorter forms of fiction; and many have written letters or kept diaries that constitute a significant part of their literary output. A brief study cannot hope to deal with all these in detail, but where the shorter fiction and the non-fictional writings, public and private, have an important relationship to the novels, some space has been devoted to them.

To Jim and Kate

1

Introduction

Between 1952 and 1955 a number of new and articulate voices in British fiction began to claim public attention. For several years before, commentators had speculated about where or what the new generation was, wondered how the Second World War might be treated in serious fiction and worried that fatigue or public austerity might have been instrumental in a premature atrophy among the potentially creative. When their fiction reached enthusiastic public notice, in the early 1950s, the work of Kingsley Amis, Iris Murdoch, John Wain, Doris Lessing, Angus Wilson (who was slightly older but did not publish a novel until 1952), Thomas Hinde and Philip Larkin (who had written two novels in the late 1940s before publishing his poetry) began to be regarded as representative of a new post-war generation. In the initial and often superficial responses to their fiction, the new voices emerging from the war seemed to many comic and limited, often insular, interested in questions of food and class, and influenced, in one way or another, by a vaguely Sartrean or existential version of experience. For good or ill, depending on the point of view, and most often for both good and ill, they did not seem to demonstrate much concern with eternal verities or transforming visions of human experience. Alone among these emerging writers, although eventually noticed nearly as much as any of them, William Golding, from the appearance of *Lord of the Flies* in 1954, was seen as a visionary dealing with universal and essential human issues, was not part of a group or a generation. Somewhat older than the others (although only two years older than Angus Wilson), Golding seemed an anomaly among the novelists of the early and middle 1950s. For some, in both England and America, Golding was immune from the dominant temper of the age, from the bland muted, non-charismatic, comic safety of

1

the carefully limited survivor; for others, Golding was both surly and reactionary, seen, as late as 1960 in an article in *The Nation* by Martin Green, as motivated by a 'sullen distaste for the contemporary'.[1]

Golding's singularity seemed confirmed by his distance from the London literary world. He was a schoolmaster teaching English and Greek literature at Bishop Wordsworth's in Salisbury, living nearby in Wiltshire in a cottage called Ebble Thatch. Forty-three years old, married, with two children, and part of no discernible literary group, Golding seemed an isolated figure to the literary public. Only gradually through the latter years of the 1950s, as his work assumed considerable prominence and generated interest in the man, did the facts of his early life begin to appear publicly.

William Gerald Golding was born in Cornwall on 19 September 1911, one of two sons born to Alec Golding, who became Senior Master at Marlborough Grammar School, and his wife, Mildred, an active worker for women's suffrage. For a time, in Marlborough, they lived next to the church graveyard. A pupil at his father's school, Golding has since frequently described his father as an overwhelming influence on his early life. In an essay entitled 'The Ladder and the Tree', Golding recalled his father as 'incarnate omniscience'. Alec wrote textbooks on various scientific subjects, including astro-physical navigation, and played at least five musical instruments: 'He could carve a mantelpiece or a jewel box, explain the calculus and the ablative absolute.'[2] As Golding has described his father, there was something almost intimidating about his omniscience and omnicompetence, as if the growing young William had little room to work out anything for himself. Alec Golding also campaigned for the Labour Party among local workmen, although apparently never himself a candidate for office. More significantly for William's future development as both person and novelist, Alec was a consummate rationalist, always learned and logical, according to his son in a series of conversations with Jack I. Biles, not 'a man who scoffed at God' but one who 'regretted God so profoundly that he almost believed in Him'.[3]

In 1930, Golding entered Brasenose College, Oxford. He had been well trained in science and had learned to play the piano, the cello, the oboe, the violin and the viola. At Oxford, he studied the sciences for two years, then switched to English

Literature, taking an additional three years to finish his degree. He was particularly interested in Anglo-Saxon. In talking with Biles, Golding has stated that he had wanted to switch from science to literature earlier, but had delayed because 'it would hurt my father so much'.[4] Golding had been interested in stories and literature since childhood, having written a play about ancient Egypt at the age of seven and begun what was planned as a twelve-volume history of the trade unions in England, reflecting the interests of his parents, at the age of twelve. At Oxford he wrote poetry. A friend of his sent a collection of his poems to Macmillan, then publishing a series of 'Contemporary Poets'. To what the later Golding has consistently maintained was his complete surprise, the editor accepted his work and twenty-nine of them were published as *Poems* on 30 October 1934. The poems justify Golding's later dismissal of them as inconsequential and adolescent. A number are rather vague, vapid and generally derivative exercises in romantic feeling. Some, like 'Vignette', satirise the confidence of the working-class rationalist storming the barricades; others, like 'Non-Philosopher's Song', work on the impossibility of reconciling the dichotomy between the worlds of 'Love' and 'Reason', heart and head. One poem depends on the culturally conventional denigration of 'Mr. Pope', the apostle of rationalism who, amidst the ordered garden, complains to God that the stars are out of line and concludes with rather laboured irony:

> If they would dance a minuet
> Instead of roaming wild and free
> Or stand in rows all trim and neat
> How exquisite the sky would be!

Poems received virtually no attention and Golding was not part of an articulate university group of poets like that of Auden, Spender, MacNeice and Day Lewis some years earlier, or that of Amis, Wain and Larkin, known as 'The Movement', some years later. When Golding offered further poems to his editor, Macmillan showed no interest.

After leaving Oxford in 1935, Golding moved to London, writing, acting and producing for a small and non-commercial theatre far from the West End. He once acted the part of Danny, the sinister scholarship boy in Emlyn Williams' *Night*

Must Fall. In 1939, Gólding married Ann Brookfield and took a position as schoolmaster at Bishop Wordsworth's School in Salisbury. He joined the Royal Navy in 1940, serving throughout the rest of the Second World War. Golding's retrospective accounts of his war-time career, in his essays and conversations, are likely to be casual and to undercut any suggestion of the heroic. He began as an ordinary seaman. In taking an examination to become an officer, he answered a question on the difference between a propellant and an explosive with such elaborate knowledge, including graphs, that he was sent almost immediately to a secret research centre under the direction of Professor Lindemann, Churchill's scientific advisor who later became Lord Cherwell. Golding reports having enjoyed doing research on explosives until he accidentally 'blew myself up'. After recovering, he requested that the Admiralty 'Send me back to sea, for God's sakes, where there's peace'. He was sent to a mine-sweeper school in Scotland, then to New York to wait for six months while a mine-sweeper was built on Long Island. By the time he returned, mine-sweepers were no longer necessary and he was given command of a small rocket-launching craft in time for the 1944 invasion of the Continent. In one invasion, that of the small Dutch island of Walcheren, Golding reports, his craft was assigned a difficult role without air support. Preparing to go through a narrow channel in which 'everybody was throwing stuff in every direction', Golding transfixed his face with a grin and his men assumed that the job could not be as dangerous as it looked because he seemed to be enjoying it so much. When orders were changed, assigning his craft a much safer function, Golding's 'grin fell off' and his face 'collapsed'. His crew said to each other, 'Do you see that old bastard up there? When he learnt we weren't going in, he was disappointed!'[5]

Of course the war lingered more deeply and crucially in Golding's mind than these anecdotes suggest. In fact, in various interviews, he has attributed the compelling quality of his subsequent fiction to the fact that during the war 'One had one's nose rubbed in the human condition'.[6] He recognised that in the past he had been naïve and adolescent, that the war had demonstrated all the horrendous cruelties of which man was capable. He took little comfort in being on the 'right' side, for he recognised that only the accident of 'certain social sanctions' or 'social prohibitions' prevented most people in the Allied countries from acting with a brutality and disregard for humanity similar to that of the Nazis. He thought many of the British and Americans after the war too complacent, too confident of their own distance from what Nazism represented. Golding's concerns, however, took considerable time to emerge in fiction. After the war, he returned to Bishop Wordsworth's and, in his spare time, wrote a number of novels he now calls 'pot-boilers' that were not published. He finally discovered a form for what he wanted to say and wrote *Lord of the Flies*. The novel was rejected by twenty-one publishers before Faber & Faber brought it out in 1954.

Although treated respectfully, sometimes even enthusiastically, in reviews, *Lord of the Flies* was not an instantaneous public success. Nevertheless, its reception encouraged Golding to follow it quickly with other similarly original and distinctive novels, *The Inheritors* published in 1955 and *Pincher Martin* in 1956. Golding has always worked in spurts of intense energy, recalling, with his wife's help, that he had written *Lord of the Flies* in three or four months, *The Inheritors* in twenty-eight days while teaching, and the first draft of *Pincher Martin* in three weeks over a Christmas holiday.[7] He still thinks over a work for a long period of time, then writes quickly. Golding's unusual fictions began to receive both more serious critical attention and wider popular acclaim, *Lord of the Flies* in particular, becoming enthusiastically read and absorbed in universities and schools in both Britain and America. *Lord of the Flies* was made into a popular film. Golding published another novel, *Free Fall*, in 1959, one that although expectantly anticipated and publicised achieved less of a public because it was different from the others. This, however, barely affected the rapid growth of Golding's public reputation. Frequent interviews, invitations and popular success led Golding to resign from his positon as a schoolmaster in 1961, travel to teach at Hollins College in Virginia for the 1961–62 academic year, work as a frequent book reviewer for *The Spectator* from 1960 to 1962, and eventually earn his living solely as a writer.

In the years since, Golding has travelled a good deal, lecturing and granting interviews. He has spent considerable time on his boat, cruising through the English Channel, the Dutch waterways, and ports along the North and Baltic Seas.

He had planned to sail to Greece in 1967, but his boat capsised after a collision in the English Channel off the Isle of Wight. He retains something of his interests in engineering and mechanics, in how things work. And, despite the fact that others have sometimes too simplistically, from his fictions, labelled him as politically conservative or reactionary, he described himself in 1970 as a non-Marxist Socialist, left of centre, '*bitterly* left of centre'.[8] Most importantly, however, he sees himself as a writer who is constantly changing and responding to his universe. As he often says, he sees no point in writing the same novel twice. In fact, his striking fictions, although of course some have some elements in common with others, are all substantially different from each other. He tends, still, to finish or to publish in spurts, although the clusters of fiction may contain novels that, at least on the surface, do not resemble each other at all. Respect for his fiction has built fairly consistently: he was elected a fellow of the Royal Society of Literature in 1955 and made a CBE in 1966. After *Free Fall*, he published the widely heralded *The Spire* in 1964 and *The Pyramid* in 1967. In 1971, he published three short novels under the title *The Scorpion God*, one of which, 'Envoy Extraordinary', had been published in 1956 in a collection, along with two novella by other writers, entitled *Sometime, Never*. 'Envoy Extraordinary' was also the basis for Golding's play, *The Brass Butterfly*, performed in both Oxford and London in 1958 with Alastair Sim in the principal role of the emperor. Golding published little during the 1970s until another burst of fictional energy manifested itself at the end of the decade. *Darkness Visible* came out in 1979 and *Rites of Passage* (which won the Booker prize for fiction) in 1980. Another novel, *The Paper Men*, was published in 1984. Golding's non-fiction, his essays on his travels, his ideas and the genesis of his fictions also seem to have emerged in the two different spurts that echo the periods of intense critical and public attention given him. *The Hot Gates and Other Occasional Pieces*, collecting the essays from the early 1960s, appeared in 1965; *A Moving Target*, comprised of pieces from the period of resurrected attention in the early 1980s, came out in 1982 and was the immediate occasion for awarding Golding the 1983 Nobel Prize for fiction. Golding has followed that with an account of his extended 1984 trip on a small boat down the Nile in *An Egyptian Journal* published in 1985.

None of his work other than *Lord of the Flies* has achieved the exciting appeal and public force of seeming to represent a generation. Yet each of the fictions is singular, original, a condensed version of human experience compressed into distinctive form. Each has also generated considerable discussion, and what Golding has seemed, at particular moments during his career, to be doing in fiction has not always been what, seen retrospectively, he in fact has done. His fictions are dense, difficult and can appeal in ways that are simpler than the complexities they reveal. His background in terms of ideas, influences and abstractions requires further exploration before possible patterns within particular novels and common to a number of the novels can more helpfully be examined.

2
Background Themes: The Propellants

Although his statements are sometimes arch or cryptic, Golding's own essays and the interviews he has given are generally the best sources for the genesis and development of his ideas. In 1970, he acknowledged that he had, in his fiction, always been an 'ideas man' rather than a 'character man', although he hoped that he might some day combine the two. He saw the concentration on 'ideas', like that in Aldous Huxley's fiction, as a 'basic defect'. Citing Angus Wilson's *The Middle Age of Mrs. Eliot* as an example of the opposite kind of fiction, he stated that he admired such fiction that could create 'fully realized, rounded, whole, believable' characters.[9] In more recent accounts, as in a 1977 lecture on his first visit to Egypt in 1976, Golding has tended to see the concentration on ideas or things at the expense of character as an accusation, which may or may not be true, that others level at his work. In this particular instance, he resolved to include character sketches in his journal.

Golding's interest in Egypt and archaeology began in childhood. As he explains in 'Egypt from My Inside', an essay first published in *The Hot Gates* and reprinted in *A Moving Target*, when he wanted, at the age of seven, to write a play about ancient Egypt, he decided to learn hieroglyphics so that his characters might speak in their appropriate language. He persisted with the symbols although the play never got very far. He also reports that, whenever his mother took him to London, he 'nagged and bullied' to visit the Egyptian mummies and papyri in the British Museum. On one occasion, Golding stood transfixed before a showcase. The curator, noticing him, asked if he would like to assist and led him to a part of the Museum

8

closed to the public to see a huge sarcophagus and help unwrap a shrouded mummy. Golding's enthusiasm for Egyptian artifacts slightly antedated the exhibition of the relics from the recently unearthed tomb of Tutankhamen that so excited London in 1922, but there is little doubt that both Golding's interest and that of the large public were imaginative responses to a whole series of archaeological discoveries in the first quarter of the twentieth century. Golding's fascination with ancient Egyptian relics continued, even though he was unable to visit the actual land for more than half a century. Inevitably, the visit was something of a disappointment. Planning to tour Egypt by car, with his wife, he was understandably distracted by the difficulties in finding hotels, the unreliability of arrangements, the dirt of travel and accommodations, the suffering from constant diarrhoea, and the 'swarm' of people. Crowds and discomfort impeded his appreciation of the Great Pyramid. Only when he and his wife joined some American tourists more knowledgeable about contemporary Egypt did he see more of the tombs and antiquities around Cairo. Something of Golding's removal from people is apparent in his description of these tourists. Although grateful for their knowledge and friendship, he concludes his account of the episode, in the essay entitled 'Egypt from My Outside', with a flatly chilling emphasis on the fact that 'I don't suppose we shall ever see each other again'.[10] Later, through these friends and others, Golding and his wife stayed at a large archaeological encampment in Luxor, run by the British and the Americans. There, with frequent guides and minimal comfort assured, he was able to explore the pyramids and other antiquities, to live within the Egyptian 'Mystery' of his imagination. His second trip, piloting the boat down the Nile in 1984, was more efficiently prepared. Even so, he found it difficult not to be distracted or appalled by the Egyptian dirt, sloth, helplessness and random violence. In trying to conclude *An Egyptian Journal*, to match the ancient with the contemporary or the imaginative with the physical reality, as well as to satisfy his commission by 'having an opinion on everything', Golding can only summarise by appealing to 'strange and nonsensical complexity' and hope that the reader can share something of the 'irritations and excitements of our absurd journey'.[11]

Egypt as a specific locus is less significant for Golding than what it represents as excavating a buried past. Growing up in

Marlborough, reading about Egyptian legends and the discoveries of tombs, cycling around Wiltshire and visiting Stonehenge, Old Sarum, and various forts and burial mounds, Golding's imagination was always archaeological. In a 1966 essay called 'Wiltshire', he discusses the combination of the survivals of the prehistoric, the Roman, the Celtic, the legendary (the grave of Merlin is said to be in the grounds of a Wiltshire school), the early Christian, the Saxon and the Norman. He concludes: 'This is antiquity on a time scale to compete with Egypt.'[12] He is also fascinated by the flowers of Wiltshire, the botanical variety, but has little interest in the touristy, manufactured medieval festivals or revivals of Morris dancing. Constructions propel Golding's imagination almost as strongly as do excavations, and the cathedral at Salisbury is an important landmark in Golding's consciousness. In an interview, Golding, asked about what research he had done in preparation for writing *The Spire*, replied that he had not needed particular research, for 'if you have lived for half a century or more in the south of England and you are naturally curious about a great many things, one of the things you're curious about is churches'. He goes on to demonstrate more than ordinary curiosity, talking of the distribution of constructive forces like an engineer and the suggestions of design like a historically sensitive architect. He has firm historical opinions as well, as in claiming that the Normans, in building their churches, 'always overplayed their hand': 'They weren't taking any risks; everything was gorillalike'.[13] In contrast, the later medieval builders combined technical knowledge with high imagination to create something like the spire of Salisbury Cathedral. In an essay in *A Moving Target*, originally written for *Holiday* magazine in 1965, called 'An Affection for Cathedrals', Golding first brings up his respect for the 'diver' who, early in the twentieth century, worked daily in the slime beneath Winchester Cathedral to underpin the walls and shore up the shaky foundations. He then contrasts this with Salisbury, with the spire, equally shaky in construction, but able to 'pull' the surrounding landscape. The spire is the nobler structure, as if all rivers and roads gather toward it as it draws the community and the landscape into an image that transcends itself. Golding recalls that, during the seventeenth-century civil war, zealots smashed the faces depicted in the Salisbury stained glass and that, at these and other times, vandals have smashed or broken off the stone noses of sculpted figures. But the spire is beyond such random and personal desecration, both as symbol and as a miracle of engineering.

Golding's sensitivity to place is by no means limited to the archaeological or to his geographical origins. Other pieces published in *A Moving Target*, for example, crystallise historical and social impressions of various other locales. 'Through the Dutch Waterways' effectively describes the 'wide light' and 'soft' sky visible on one of Golding's boat trips with his family. Canals lead to a 'huddle' of houses 'with a golden crown hanging over them'; the bridges that control squat traffic so calmly are structures of 'delicate elegance'. The light and sky, the 'defined luminosities', combine with the 'mudpats' of islands and the engineering marvels of the canals to create what Golding sees as a 'poetry of order'.[14] Another piece called 'Delphi' connects the harsh and remote landscape with the oracles and Gods of ancient Greece. Ancient Greece, in fact, is frequently central to Golding's imagination. He studied Greek while in the Navy during the war, initially, he has stated, to help pass the dull hours on watch. Although most of the Greek literature he has taught has been Greek in English translation, Greek myths and symbols infuse his novels. The essay from *The Hot Gates* that gives the collection its title describes his visit to the mountains of Thessaly and the Pass of Thermopylae, where Golding, climbing the cliffs, recalls his sense of peril: 'I stayed there, clinging to a rock . . . I was clinging to Greece herself'.[15] The locus and the connection recall the principal metaphor of *Pincher Martin*, a novel which can also be read as a suggestive and expanded retelling of the Aeschylean version of Prometheus chained to a rock by the Gods as punishment for his *hubris*.

Sometimes, Golding's use of Greece is referential and mythical, a saturation in the culture that gives him material for the creation of his own metaphorical statements about the human condition (and he has, at moments, thought of his work as attempts to create myths for contemporary man). At other times, however, the idea of Greece functions as a significant contrast to the idea of Egypt in Golding's imagination. Golding establishes a polarity of historical and cultural influence, contrasting the rationalism and light associated with the Greek tradition with the mystery and the darkness, swaddled in a mummy-like unknown that he has always connected with the

Egyptian tradition and its appeal. In 'Egypt from My Inside', after giving the facts of his early attraction to Egyptian artifacts, he talks of his fascination with mystery as a child, regarding the fascination as something quite different from trying rationally to work out the puzzle. He saw his attraction to the artifacts as an attraction to darkness, to mystery with no solution. In retrospect, he can see what has persisted from childhood as feeling himself linked to the Egyptian's 'unreason, spiritual pragmatism and capacity for ambiguous and even contradictory belief'.[16] In *An Egyptian Journal*, he conveys the polarity in more referential literary terms. He begins the book by explaining his sixty-year attachment to ancient Egypt as an attraction to its 'immobility' amidst change. This is the quality visible in the fiction of Rider Haggard, full of adventure, contradiction and mystery. The rational and puzzle-solving is represented by the Sherlock Holmes fiction. As a child, and still (although he realises that the fiction bears little resemblance to reality), Golding preferred Rider Haggard.

The polarity between the rational and the imaginative or mysterious is always visible in all Golding's work, a consistency that balances the variety of the location of experience in particular different places. The locations, the places, are the tangible moments of particular intensity, while the polarity itself, the constant opposition of the rationally understandable and the mysterious in human experience, is the nature of all human experience. In ways, the polarity reflects Golding's early consciousness of experience, and can be connected to both his desire to separate himself from the father he regarded as 'incarnate omniscience' and his switch at Oxford from doing sciences to doing literature. But Golding also sees the polarity as universal, as a permanent quality that justifies its compressed elaborations in the novels. Although he always values most the side more difficult to apprehend, the mysterious or imaginative, the dark side, he never oversimplifies the issue, never, for example, abandons his interest in and respect for engineering, as, even in the midst of his rebellion and self-definition, he never lost his considerable respect and affection for his father. Yet within the fictional dramatisations of varieties of the polarity, varieties that reveal his constantly interesting and imaginative mind, he does see the two sides of experience as identifiably separate, as pressures that pull the human being in different directions and comprise a constant source of human pain.

As he has indicated in interviews, Golding thinks we live constantly in 'two worlds', one physical and the other spiritual, and that the experience of the 'two worlds' is basically emblematic of our nature. As he explained in his defence of the title for *Free Fall*, he thinks the 'model intellectual' is 'literally in this state of free fall' both in terms of theology and in terms of science. The theology underlines man's suspension between the base 'physical' and the elevated 'spiritual', the science reflects man floating in a universe in which 'gravity has *gone*'.[17] For Golding, who most often uses the conventional religious terms, 'physical' and 'spiritual', to identify the polarity, the 'physical' is equated with the rational. He sees the rational view of experience as denying the irrational, the mysterious, or the 'spiritual'. Yet, for Golding, the 'spiritual' is always felt, always there. And the polarity leads, in Golding's perspective, to the constant 'dissociation of thought and feeling'.[18] Golding has often said that he has no solution to the dissociation, no 'bridge' between the worlds of thought and feeling. And he has always been interested in the thought of people he regards as seers, like Rudolf Steiner, whose cosmology attempts to combine the scientific and the religious. While Golding has not, at least publicly, committed himself to any particular theoretical 'bridge', he has repeatedly expressed his faith that some sort of 'bridge' between the two separate worlds exists. The compressed metaphors of Golding's fictions are most frequently attempts to synthesise the constant problem or to suggest a plausible 'bridge'.

Seeing human experience in terms of a basic polarity, of physical and spiritual worlds or of thought and feeling, is a frequent corollary of a religious perspective. The polarity between the physical and the spiritual, for example, dominates various forms of religious Puritanism, a theology in which the various claims of the physical being must be suppressed or denied in order to ensure the claims of the spiritual for salvation. Puritanism postulates an inverse relationship between the two, as if the human being has a finite amount of energy and spending less in one world will guarantee a richer expenditure in the other. For most Puritans, sex represents the threat of physical waste, the profligate expenditure that will leave little

energy for the possibility of spiritual salvation. Golding's version
of the two worlds, however, is different from this. Sexuality is
not always stigmatised as simply physical – in fact, at times,
sexuality becomes a tangible means for exploring a world of
richer and more rewarding imagination. As he has often said in
interviews, Golding thinks sex is sinful only when it is exploitive.
His fiction is full of graphic descriptions of waste, of the
functions of excretion. Many of the novels, like *Lord of the Flies*,
The Spire and *The Pyramid* connect excretion with the limitations
of rationalism or dwell on it as an example of the loathsome
inferiority of the being immersed in the sole realm of the
physical. Mud, slime, faeces, waste of all sorts are points of
focus in Golding's fictional landscapes, which often seem to
resemble a massive lavatory. As in Swift's similar fiction, the
excremental also suggests ugliness, moral failure, depravity and
inadequacy. In the words of the critics Bernard S. Oldsey and
Stanley Weintraub, Golding's Swiftian 'obsession' illustrates
his 'dung-heap-and-rose principle of beauty'.[19] His two worlds
are morally and aesthetically far apart, and 'bridges' are
difficult to build. In Golding's more recent literal accounts of
experience, as in recording his trips to Egypt, he emphasises
mud and excretion almost as much as he does in his fiction,
commenting frequently on the barely operative lavatories on
the boat, the Nile as sewer, and the rarely achieved ideal of a
bath in fresh water. Here, however, instead of representing the
rational, the excretory and the physical are irrational, connected
with the bad engineering of all those unfinished bridges across
the Nile. Despite his constant use of polarities to represent the
pains and problems of human experience, Golding never allows
a falsifying and abstract consistency to distort the complexity of
experience he visualises and presents.

Golding's polarities are not illustrations of particular doctrine
or attitude; rather, they are shaped carefully to reflect the
complicated nature of the human being. In his fiction, he uses
his knowledge of the ancient Greeks, of engineering, of English
literature, of Egyptian civilisation, and of a whole chain of ideas
about human sin and goodness implicit within the Western
Christian tradition, to condense his sense of the human condition
into essence. Unlike most of his contemporaries writing in the
1950s, Amis, Wain, Wilson and Lessing, Golding was not
primarily interested in issues of society or class, issues about the

relationships between people all of whom he depicted and accepted as fallible. In the works of others, human beings lived, temporised, sorted themselves out by choice in equivocal relationships that were seen as partial or comic, as if no absolute or universal statement could ever be made about the nature of man. In contrast, Golding saw man as finally and inherently wicked. As he has said when interviewed, 'The basic point my generation discovered about man was that there was more evil in him that could be accounted for simply by social pressures.'[20] Although over the last twenty-five years Golding has come to deal with issues of society and class, has extended the forms and the concerns of his fiction, his sense of an inexpungeable evil or darkness in man remains. His most copious recent social novel is called *Darkness Visible*, and, like most of his others, it compresses a great deal of human material into a metaphor for human evil and bestiality.

The concentration on darkness is also necessarily a concentration on light. Golding never attenuates his seriousness or his drama by any complacent satisfaction in the darkness of the human condition. In seeing the human being as 'morally diseased', as he said in 'The Hot Gates', Golding has tried to use his fiction to suggest possible counterweights to the human condition. If man is evil and is not socially perfectible, not perfectible by any of the measures taken by or the illusions of the conscious and rational society, Golding often suggests, at the fringes of his fiction, what 'light' might mean in contrast to the prevailing human 'darkness'. His work is, as he sees it, constantly moral, concerned with which 'light' might locate the 'darkness', what consciousness might put human experience in a more serious, profound and accurate perspective. His early novels have been defined frequently enough as fables (a complicated definition that applies in some instances more than in others and that requires examination in the terms of specific novels), and Golding has sometimes accepted the definition in so far, as he said in his essay called 'Fable' in *The Hot Gates*, as it carries the recognition that 'The fabulist is a moralist', one who, either implicitly or explicitly, didactically propounds a 'lesson' or instruction about the human condition.[21] At other times, Golding has been more hesitant about accepting the term 'fable' for his work. As he said in a well-known interview with Frank Kermode on the BBC in 1959, he would regard it as a 'tremendous compliment' were someone to substitute the word 'myth' for 'fable' in describing his work because 'myth is a much profounder and more significant thing than a fable . . . something which comes out from the roots of things in the ancient sense of being the key to existence, the whole meaning of life.'[22] Golding never claims to have achieved such significance, only to have attempted it and to have suggested its possible moral components. Some early Golding critics, like Samuel Hynes, ducked the issue of definition involved in distinguishing 'fable' from 'myth' and referred more simply and safely to Golding's 'moral models'.[23] The 'models' are necessary in that the fiction gives the morality coherent form.

Golding's moral didacticism, like the tightness of his fictional forms, has eased somewhat over the last two decades. In a 1980 talk called 'Belief and Creativity', published in *A Moving Target*, Golding has asserted that *Lord of the Flies* yields perhaps too easily 'to explication, to instruction, to the trephining of the pupil's skull by the teacher and the insertion into the pupil's brain by the teacher of what the pupil ought to think about it.' Although he has become less didactic since, he thinks 'in general terms I would still assent to the philosophical or theological implications about the nature of man and the universe presented in the book.' Golding asserts that all his novels attempt to deal with the essential human condition, with 'man at an extremity, man tested like a building material, taken into the laboratory and used to destruction; man isolated, man obsessed, man drowning in a literal sea or in the sea of his own ignorance.'[24] Convinced that the writer must describe the indescribable, the mystery of the human essence, Golding sees his statements about the human being as fundamentally religious. Yet he follows no particular religious doctrine, is in fact sceptical of all doctrines and systems, just as he finds, in their systems and in the images those systems create, Marx, Darwin and Freud 'the three most crashing bores of the Western world'.[25] Golding is always likely to be dismissive of other's icons, of any concept that replaces the size and scale of what he thinks of as God. He believes in a God that is beyond the triviality of man, not a God as 'confident authority' or system, but God as a principle of universal creation. Modern life, and particularly the theorists like Marx, Darwin and Freud, has glorified man and consequently ignored or reduced the concept of God: 'We have diminished the world of God and man in a universe ablaze with all the glories that contradict that diminution.'[26] The polarities or dichotomies within which man struggles or strangles himself are all signs of human incapacity and ignorance, for 'Truth is single'.[27] The divisions, the complexities, and the polarities of human experience are multiple evidence of human triviality and pettiness, of human distance from God.

Golding is, however, a believer and a writer with a unique and interesting mind, not a systematic theologian or a preacher. He thinks that lyric poetry, in its possible crystallisations of essence through metaphor, is likely to reflect something closer to religious belief or truth than is narrative prose. Yet the novelist also tries to approach religious truth, 'a kind of diver' searching the mud and depths of experience 'looking for a theme'.[28] In his talks and essays, in which the primary subject is most likely to be his writing, his religious impulses embedded within and only hesitantly emerging from accounts of the writing, he is usually deferential about the role of the writer. In more recent essays, he has been even less likely than he was earlier to accept for himself definitions of forms like 'fable' or 'myth'. In 'A Moving Target', as in some other recent essays, he regards himself as a teller of stories, calling the novel a 'story which is in part a fiction'. He wonders to what extent stories really have 'themes' of any importance and questions what value such themes might have. In retrospect, he thinks that *Lord of the Flies* 'has either no theme or all theme', and, after giving an account of both the personal and the generational circumstances of its genesis, concludes that he now sees its theme, found through the novel, as 'grief, sheer grief, grief, grief, grief'.[29] In contrast, *The Inheritors* was written to the intellectual specification of a theme already thought through. Subsequent novels, in their variety, have illustrated other versions of the relationship between 'story' and 'theme' or meaning. And Golding is honestly searching and unprogrammatic in trying to account for the various ways in which meaning or that singular truth behind or beneath experience may or may not emerge from the stories he wants to tell.

Golding is also the writer in developing a good deal of his self-definition through the literature of others, illustrating the fact that literature more than abstract ideas serves as the knowable source for his perspectives. He often goes back to his initial love for poetry. In a 1981 essay called 'My First Book', after citing the irony that his slim volume of thirty-four pages of poetry, remaindered in 1934, was worth $4000 in the United States in 1981, he talks of all the attention given to reciting poetry at the dame school he attended when he was a child. The recitations gave him an interest in 'interior stance', in simple lyrics, and in the vocative like 'Oh!' and 'Ah!' This helped him to feel poetry as something closer to singular truth, to the emotions of what simply transcends, a kind of poetry far from intellectualised, intricately complex and dichotomous 'aberrations like metaphysical poetry'. He thinks of his poetry as having no concern with social issues, no interest in progressive reform or in the values of social amelioration with which he was brought up. Rather, he calls his poetry 'conservative and anarchist, in so far as it can be described in social terms at all. As a poet, however, his closest identification is with the poetry of Tennyson, which he has always loved although he knew, even as a young man, that it was very much out of fashion. Although Golding grants that Tennyson's poetry, like his own, 'lacked intellectual mobility', he found, in some of Tennyson's lyrics, the singular voice, the 'interior stance' and the purity of evocative sound that he thought closest to the human expression of truth.[30]

In a less pure and singular manner, Golding also defines something of himself as writer through the fiction of others. In a 1977 talk called 'Rough Magic', he described some of the fictional practices and conventions that had influenced him. He used a passage from *Wuthering Heights*, one of wild emotion generated from slight and unconvincing detail, the 'splashes of blood' when Heathcliff dashes his head against a tree, to illustrate what Golding calls 'badly written, implausible, ridiculous'. More positively, he uses Dickens, the pithy compression of Jane Austen in sentences in which the carefully controlled irony might be seen as going in several different directions, and the tentative although 'extraordinary strength' of Henry James's narration. Golding also appreciates the natural rhythms and 'sheer daring' in John Steinbeck's prose – an interesting identification in the light of some subsequent exterior identifications when Golding won his Nobel Prize and numbers of critics complained that, like Steinbeck, he did not deserve it. Sometimes, Golding's quotations from others seem eccentric or out of context – he never follows any version of a standard or canonical apprehension of English literature. He wrenches T. S. Eliot's statement that mankind cannot bear too much reality into an elitist scorn for the common man, a distortion that Golding can then, too simply, define himself against. Yet he also does appreciate some of Eliot's verse, and uses him as an example of a writer who can sometimes create a 'higher language', a form of language that both creates and achieves significant mystery.[31] For Golding, in both poetry and prose, art inheres in the language and the form that elicits the mysterious, the truth so singular and simple in itself yet so difficult for man to find, to know, or to express.

3

The Fictional Explosion:
Lord of the Flies and
The Inheritors

Given the complexity of Golding's thought, his need to express some fundamental statement about the nature of man in tangible terms, and his tendency to use sharply defined polarities to generate his ideas, his placement of his first two novels as intellectual responses to particular targets is not surprising. His religious impulse requires a heresy or an evil to excoriate; the pressure of his carefully shaped and internal fiction gains its force in reaction against some widely shared or familiar concept. Both the first two novels focus on their targets explicitly: *Lord of the Flies* on R. M. Ballantyne's 1857 novel *The Coral Island*, *The Inheritors* on H. G. Wells's *Outline of History*.

Ballantyne's *The Coral Island* represents, for Golding, an extremity of Victorian confidence and optimism in the civilised values of English schoolboy society. In Ballantyne's novel, the boys, shipwrecked on the island, organise their skills and exercise their imaginations to duplicate the comforts and the values of the society they have temporarily lost. Working with discipline, they build shelters and a boat, make various utensils for their convenience, and find a healthy and interesting variety of animal and vegetable food. With the same kind of devotion to higher powers that characterises the more adult survival in the earlier *Robinson Crusoe*, the boys in *The Coral Island* radiate a confidence in their sense of community and organisation which would seem rather smug were they not also genuinely pious and aware of their luck. Evil in the novel is externalised, represented by cannibals on the island whom the English boys defeat because they work together and excel in both wit and virtue. Their rescue almost does not matter, for they have essentially recreated the world they came from. Ballantyne draws on a concept of the child that reaches back through the nineteenth century, at least as far as Rousseau and Locke, the child as inherently either good or neutral, manifesting his goodness if left alone and uncorrupted by the adult world or reflecting and recreating the healthy and civilised environment of his initial consciousness. This confidence in civilised Enlightenment, developed from a faith in human possibility in the eighteenth century to a particularly English social achievement in the nineteenth, is precisely what Golding, in *Lord of the Flies*, is determined to reverse. The locus of Golding's attention is the society of boys; the implication is an attack on the naïveté of Victorian confidence in English boys and in public schools, as well as on the whole Enlightenment doctrine about the progress and perfectibility of the human species. Golding's tone, however, is not that of triumphant response to a naïve and mistaken ideology. Rather, his shaping of events and experience on the island, his sense of the inherently predatory and evil characteristics his boys reveal, is dominated by the 'grief, sheer grief' he called the theme of the novel. The 'grief' compounds the presentation of 'sin', for, as Golding has said retrospectively as recently as December 1985, the novel was 'written at a time of great world grief' and that, in addition to the 'original sin' latent in the novel, 'what nobody's noticed is that it also has original virtue'.[32]

Golding's use of *The Coral Island* is direct and unambiguous. He refers to it explicitly several times: once, near the beginning of the novel, when the boys, in momentary agreement, decide they can have a 'good time on this island', like 'Treasure Island', and 'Coral Island'; later, on the last page of the novel, ironically, when they are rescued by the naval officer, who imperceptively comments, 'Jolly good show. Like the Coral Island'. Golding also derives the initial English types of some of his schoolboy characters from Ballantyne's novel. The narrator of *The Coral Island* is named Ralph, a sound and stable boy of 15 (his last name is Rover); the strongest, oldest, tallest boy is named Jack; the third member of Ballantyne's principal triumvirate is Peterkin Gay, a quick, sprite-like, imaginative boy of 14. Golding's Ralph comes closest to following the Ballantyne model, for Ralph, although not the narrator in

Golding, is the centrally representative English schoolboy, simultaneously the one who both leads and accommodates to others in terms of the fondly cherished, moderate English tradition. Fair-haired, mild, neither the strongest nor the most discerning of the boys, Golding's Ralph is initially elected to govern the island and to organise building shelters and possible rescue. As the organisation increasingly breaks down, as the boys gradually succumb to dirt, ineptitude, laziness, cruelty and the predatory viciousness of the 'hunters', Ralph reveals something of the same sense of inherent evil within himself (he willingly shares the spoils of the 'hunters' and, however reluctantly and unconsciously, joins in the ritualistic killing of Simon). Finally, hunted by the others, turned from leader into victim, his 'rescue' at the end is far from any reassertion of his moderation. At the end he 'weeps', his confidence shattered, recognising the failure and the irrelevance of the kind of human moderation and civilisation he had thought he embodied. Golding changes the Ballantyne version of the character of Jack, the powerful one outside the communal structure, more immediately and more markedly than that of Ralph. In the first place, Golding's Jack has his own community, his choir of 'hunters', each boy wearing 'a square black cap with a silver badge in it': 'Their bodies, from throat to ankle, were hidden by black cloaks which bore a long silver cross on the left breast and each neck was finished off with a hambone frill' (Chapter I). The physical description deliberately suggests the Nazis, the sense of inherent evil institutionalised and made visible in the chanting choir of the predatory. Ballantyne's Jack represented strength absorbed into the civilised community and displayed no sense of evil; Golding's Jack is the aggressive force of evil, acquiring more and more adherents as survival on the island becomes progressively more difficult. Jack imposes a sense of discipline on the others that Ralph can never manage.

The character of Piggy, Ralph's most loyal supporter, is entirely Golding's addition. Physically deficient (he is fat, asthmatic and has a weak bladder), Piggy is the voice of rationalism. He believes in the possibility of rescue by the adult society, in the values of civilisation, and in the possibility of directing human constructive effort. Normally less articulate than Ralph, attempting to endow the symbol of the conch shell, the parliamentary symbol, with silent power, Piggy, in his final

scene, eventually poses, to the assembled boys on the pinnacle
rock at the end of the island, a series of rhetorical questions
that represent his values. He advocates that the boys 'be
sensible like Ralph is', 'have rules and agree', and follow 'law
and rescue', rather than follow Jack and 'hunt and kill'
(Chapter XI). In response, Roger, Jack's most vicious lieutenant,
high overhead, uses a boulder as a lever to hurl the rock that
hits Piggy, casts him forty feet down to hit another rock that
splatters his brains before he is washed out to sea. In his death
'Piggy's arms and legs twitched a bit, like a pig's after it has
been killed', and Roger had leaned his weight on the lever in
the same way he had earlier leaned his weight on his spear to
kill the sow. Piggy is the human object, the victim, for the
predators. Yet the rationalism and confidence in social
organisation does not summarise the function of Piggy's
character entirely. He is also fearful, not of the 'beast' the
'littluns' fear, for, unlike the 'littluns', who experience only
chaos once they forget the superficial and carefully taught
names, addresses and telephone numbers of identity, Piggy
believes in scientific observation, in tracing patterns of cause
and effect. Rather, Piggy is frightened of the 'beast' within the
human being, of people themselves. When, at the end of the
novel, Ralph weeps for 'the end of innocence, the darkness of
man's heart, and the fall through the air of the true, wise friend
called Piggy', the sense of Piggy's wisdom is not an endorsement
of Piggy's rationalism or his science. Rather, Piggy's wisdom,
despite all his manifest inadequacies, consisted in his knowing
what to fear, in his accurate location of the human evil he
attracts and can do nothing to prevent.

Piggy is not the only scapegoat for the human choir's evil, for
both the rationalist and the visionary, both Piggy and Simon,
are destroyed. Simon is considerably transformed from the
model of Ballantyne's sprite-like Peterkin. In the 1959 interview
with Frank Kermode, broadcast as 'The Meaning of it All',
Golding directly indicated how he changed Peterkin into Simon
(citing the New Testament transformation of 'Simon called
Peter') and endowed the sensitive, isolated character, unlike the
other boys, with insight into the unchanging nature of human
beings and communities. Simon is mystic, unable to express
what he always knows is man's essential illness. He is Golding's
example of 'original virtue' in the novel. Yet he isolates himself,

building his shelter hidden away within the jungle, gathering the leaves and fronds he finds as a natural protection against humanity. Simon, the only one of the boys to approach closely enough to understand what they fear, actually sees the 'beast' and recognises that the 'beast' is a dead man from the war outside and above the island, his corpse tangled in his failed parachute. His recognition, in a forcefully described scene, goes more deeply than the specific circumstances demand, for it is the 'ancient, inescapable recognition' that, with the 'white teeth and dim eyes, the blood' and that 'black blob of flies that buzzed like a saw' on the 'pile of guts', the 'beast' is humanity (Chapter VIII). Simon imagines the 'beast', 'The Lord of the Flies', as a schoolmaster. Running to proclaim his discovery to the others, Simon stumbles into the pig run down the mountainside while the others, led by the choir, are enacting a ritual of 'kill the pig'. In the rush of predatory emotion, identities are confused and the 'hunters', even Ralph and Piggy drawn to the fringes of the dark and crowded scene 'under the threat of the sky', kill Simon. Simon assumes something of the role of Christ, a Christian martyrdom, sacrifice of self for the truth that is generally unrecognised. Yet Golding's symbolism is suggestive rather than precise. Like the conch, the shell that cannot support the excessive reliance on it as a parliamentary symbol and becomes worn and bleached white like a skull, the Christian symbolism is pervasive and dramatic but does not cohere in the patterns of Christian parable or duplication of the story of Christ. Simon is his own sort of visionary religious martyr, sometimes seen as more Cassandra-like than Christian, sometimes perhaps as epileptic with his fainting fits, sometimes simply as the odd boy who does not fit the pattern of the school. Similarly complex, 'The Lord of the Flies' is a translation of Beelzebub, the Greek transliteration of the ancient Hebrew word for the Prince of the Devils, an incarnation of evil in both Judaism and Christianity. Yet the figure is also characterised as the 'Lord of Dung', of human refuse. The meanings do not contradict, and both reinforce the pervasive meaning of a symbolic dramatisation of inherent human evil. Yet the cluster of symbolic meanings, both humanly and religiously suggestive, coherent only in the force and tangibility of their metaphorical application to the human condition, make it difficult to push the novel into the total narrative and legendary coherence of parable.

A reading of *Lord of the Flies* as parable is also questionable because of the way in which Golding handles time, space and location. The particular setting, graphically described physically yet unconnected to any knowable geographical location, both invites parabolic or symbolic reading in its absence from specific location and limits or questions that reading in the absence of a consistent narrative of symbolic pattern. The island is described with immediate physical force, Golding providing a strongly visual and emotional sense of the beach, the lagoon, the jungle-like tracks to the mountain, and the splinters of precipitous rock at the end of the island opposite from the lagoon. The description of the island does not substantially change, and all the elements are used symbolically, yet a pattern of meaning never coheres from the details. The only coherence is in the implications of illusion or mistaken perception, as when Ralph initially describes the island 'like icing ... on a pink cake' (Chapter I). The geography is always physical and immediate as it simultaneously renders emotional states and ideas, but geography as a coherent entity does not serve to locate parabolic narrative, as would, for example, the desert or the sea in a Biblical parable. Similarly, although the novel describes events moving through time, attention to the fire lighted for rescue gradually subsiding, the claims of the instincts of the 'hunters' rising, and the fragile identities of the 'littluns' evaporating, Golding provides no clock sense, no particular indication of how many or how quickly days or weeks pass. Images of light and dark, day and night, suggest time both physically and symbolically, but the possibility of parabolic coherence through narrative is limited by the vagueness concerning any of our usual temporal increments of days or weeks. We find it difficult to apply any specific sense of change as gradual revelation through narrative. Anticipating *Pincher Martin* in a way, Golding has wrenched usual concepts of time and space away from familiar or conventional patterns.

The force of *Lord of the Flies* emerges less from any form, like parable, than from the strength, immediacy and suggestiveness of the prose Golding writes. He is always a strikingly visual writer, evoking physical sensation. The ritualistic killing of

Simon, for example, is powerfully graphic, as the 'crowd . . . leapt on to the beast, screamed, struck, bit, tore. There were no words, and no movements but the tearing of teeth and claws.' As Simon dies from the beating, Golding shifts his attention from the fiery 'hunters' to the victim: 'The line of his cheek silvered and the turn of his shoulder became sculptured marble . . . The body lifted a fraction of an inch from the sand and a bubble of air escaped from the mouth with a wet plop.' A further shift transforms the scene to the cosmic:

> Somewhere over the darkened curve of the world the sun and moon were pulling; and the film of water on the earth planet was held, bulging slightly on one side while the solid core turned. The great wave of the tide moved further along the island and the water lifted . . . . Simon's dead body moved out toward the open sea. (Chapter IX)

As this passage illustrates, Golding's prose is a remarkable blend of the abstract and the concrete, or, more accurately perhaps, a gesture toward the abstract and symbolic through a strongly visual use of the concrete, the water 'bulging slightly on one side while the solid core turned'. Such passages build structurally in *Lord of the Flies*, connecting the abstract with the concrete in developing, for example, the symbol of the 'beast' and moving it more and more into the centre of the human creature, or in paralleling the dissipation of the echoes of civilisation with the movement toward the human interior. The constancy of the concrete prose holds the variously symbolic novel together.

The linear movement of the novel, the progress of the narration, is symbolically directed toward the human interior, stripping away what Golding sees as the falsity of confidence in civilisation, the representative illusions of Ballantyne, as the novel moves toward its fictional conclusion. References from the very beginning indicate the point of view that sees the story as the process of the gradual erosion of meaning in the paraphernalia of civilisation. On the first page of the novel, before he is even named, Ralph is described in a way that signals a sharp juxtaposition between character and setting: 'The fair boy stopped and jerked his stockings with an automatic gesture that made the jungle seem for a moment like the Home Counties.' Questions about possible rescue are asked from the beginning, sometimes with an underlying confidence, sometimes with the fear that the atomic war has expunged all potential rescuers. Throughout most of the novel, Golding plays the intimations of rescue both ways. At times, the boys' inertia and incompetence seem to prevent rescue, as when they allow the signal fire to go out, see a passing ship that does not stop, and permit their cries for rescue to be drowned out by the ritualistic chant of the choir. At other times, especially when probing the nature of the human creature, the concept of rescue seems trivial and irrelevant. When Roger is first throwing stones near another boy and only 'the taboo of the old life' prevents him from aiming to hit the boy directly, a restraint that will soon disappear, Golding writes that 'Roger's arm was conditioned by a civilisation that knew nothing of him and was in ruins' (Chapter IV). The boys become increasingly dirty as the chants of the choir become louder and more atavistic. The feeble rationalist, Piggy, becomes more and more the butt, a link between the echoes of the only superficially civilised schoolboy's world where he 'was the centre of social derision so that everyone felt cheerful and normal' (Chapter IX) and the island world with none of the veneer of civilisation in which his spectacles are smashed as a dramatic prelude to his total destruction. The twins, 'Samneric', mutually redundant, the last holdouts against the choir apart from Piggy and Ralph, 'protested out of the heart of civilisation' (Chapter XI) just before they were forced to yield to Jack and his 'hunters'. The perspective is rather like that of Conrad's *Heart of Darkness*, a progressive stripping away of the faint echoes of civilisation as the narrative moves toward its conclusion in the centre of human darkness, although Golding refuses, in this novel, to defend Conrad's final palliative of the necessary 'lie'. Golding's perspective is also suffused with human guilt for all those intelligent and rational social constructions, all those various forms of spectacles, that have been unable to overcome or assuage the central darkness.

The directed perspective, moving through narrative time, and its symbolically conveyed moral implications have invited many readers and critics to see *Lord of the Flies* in terms of parable – or, rather, since parable suggests a Biblical or Christian orthodoxy that does not fit the novel, in terms of fable. Fable is also a more useful term than parable in that the religious sources of Golding's imagination are Greek as well as Christian, echoes of the conflict between the Dionysian and the Apollonian or of Euripidean tragedy that Golding has acknowledged. The term 'fable' was first introduced to account for Golding's fictions in an essay by John Peter in 1957, Peter defining fables as 'those narratives which leave the impression that their purpose was anterior, some initial thesis or contention which they are apparently concerned to embody and express in concrete terms.' Peter distinguished the fictional fable, like Orwell's *1984*, from the novel or non-fabulistic fiction like D. H. Lawrence's *The Rainbow*. For Peter, 'the coherence of the fable appears to us as a moral tool, and its patterns become precepts', and this quality distinguished Golding's work from the dearth of value in the fiction of his contemporaries in the 1950s.[33] Later critics, writing in the 1960s, such as Bernard Oldsey and Stanley Weintraub, and Mark Kinkead-Weekes and Ian Gregor, rightly saw 'fable' as too restrictive a term for what Golding was doing. They saw his fiction as too complex and various to be reducible to conclusive moral thesis or to yield to the connection of each important physical detail with a symbolic correlative. Yet 'fable', as a term that was frequently discussed and that still is useful as a means of initiating discussion about *Lord of the Flies*, cannot entirely be ignored.

Golding himself gave the term initial critical credibility by rather equivocally accepting it in so far as 'the fabulist is the moralist' and he always saw himself as the latter. He recognised that the term was not quite right for either the range or the structure of his fiction. In terms of range and suggestability, he said, he aimed for the larger and looser dimensions of 'myth', recognising how difficult and problematic it is to try to create comprehensive myths for one's own contemporaries. In terms of structure, he thought, somewhat humbly, that he reversed some of the implications of linear fable with 'gimmicks' at the ends of his novels. Critics initially often took him at his word: some elevated his work to 'myth', others complained that the 'gimmick' reversed, reduced or palliated the fiction. In perhaps the fullest account of 'fable' as it applies to *Lord of the Flies*, John S. Whitley quotes Golding as saying that where his fable 'splits at the seams' he would like to think the split is the result of a 'plentitude of imagination'.[34] But Whitley, in his careful analysis of the form and his recognition of all the possible adaptations of 'fable', points to all Golding's intrusions, his gestures toward establishing the form and withdrawing from it, realising that the question of 'plenitude' or paucity of imagination is less the point than is the fact that fabulistic form cannot really account for the range of Golding's coherence and appeal. Golding's proportions do not fit his ostensible structure.

The problem of the 'fable' is particularly acute at the end of *Lord of the Flies* in the 'rescue' that, in moral terms, is not really a rescue. A naval officer arrives on the island to pick up the boys and saves Ralph literally from the chanting choir of 'hunters' that destroyed Piggy. Yet the naval officer is as impercipient a representative of the civilised as is any voice of Ballantyne's, for he says, on the final page of the novel, 'I should have thought that a pack of British boys – you're all British aren't you? – would have been able to put up a better show than that', and he still thinks *The Coral Island* an appropriate parallel. Besides, the naval officer is part of the wider world involved in atomic war. The atomic war generated the novel in the first place, was the device to bring the evacuated schoolboys to the island (in this sense, the boys have only duplicated the adult world), and, in the ship and the dead parachutist who is the 'Lord of the Flies', the 'Lord of Dung', and Beelzebub, the war impinges at points throughout the whole novel. Ralph has come to understand something of this, to recognise the central evil of human experience, although he does survive, and Golding, in the final line of the novel, grants him a mysteriously equivocal stance in 'allowing his eyes to rest on the trim cruiser in the distance' without comment. In terms of meaning, symbol and morality, the implications of Golding's perspective are clear: the central darkness and evil the boys revealed reflects a larger human darkness and evil, not only a violation of confidence in what the English public school represents, but also a world at war violating the false confidence of progressive and civilised values. In terms of structure and plot, in terms that 'fable' as comprehensive form would satisfy, the conclusion of the novel (as well as some earlier intrusions) violates the structural expectation that the form should be able to carry all of the novel's meaning. As Whitley sees, this is less a matter of palliative 'gimmick', has fewer of the associations of undercutting or trickery than that term suggests, than the literarily conventional resolution of the plot through a 'deus ex machina'. The form adds a 'deus ex machina' to the fable; the meaning does not require one.

Suggestive as it is for provisional examination, the term 'fable' cannot account for the extraordinarily strong feeling of coherence in Golding's novel. Rather, the coherence is visible in the distinctive and effective language, the explosive pressure of the unique and constant connection between the abstract and concrete. Coherence is also visible in Golding's perspective, his constant probing of civilised illusion, his constant stripping away of facile assurance as he approaches the evil and details the 'grief' he finds central to human experience. These are strong and appealing matters of linguistic and thematic coherence, creations of a world in fiction. The concentrated pressure of Golding's prose also creates an expectation of or hope for formal coherence as well. If, ultimately, 'truth is single', a reader looks for the singular truth in Golding's form as well. And 'fable' is a good term for the kind of formal coherence closest to what Golding is doing. Yet because of Golding's complexity, 'plenitude' or paucity of imagination as it might be, 'fable' is too centred on plot and does not entirely carry the meaning. Golding's sense of formal achievement is not fully satisifed, as it is in some of the later novels. His form, in so far as it is entirely coherent, is conditioned still by the form against which he reacts, the model of Ballantyne's *The Coral Island*. The negative form, the target, provides the points of coherence that a reading as 'fable' cannot quite sustain.

Golding's next novel, *The Inheritors*, reveals a similar formal pattern, as well as a similar interest in exploring the inner nature of the human being. The intellectual target that generates Golding's imagination in this instance is H. G. Wells's *Outline of History*, a passage from which Golding quotes as an epigraph. Elaborating on Wells's prose by including that of someone else he quotes, Golding cites a passage describing Neanderthal man, the human being's evolutionary progenitor, as repulsively strange, short, inferior to man and ugly, 'gorilla-like monsters, with cunning brains, shambling gait, hairy bodies, strong teeth, and possibly cannibalistic tendencies', which 'may be the germ of the ogre in folklore'. This passage alone is, to some extent, a simplification of Wells's point of view, for the balance of *Outline of History* is not quite so confident of human superiority in every moral and aesthetic respect as the quotation itself might suggest. Wells recognised how little we know about Neanderthal man and emphasised evolutionary change and adaptation rather than intrinsic human superiority. Nevertheless, Golding uses Wells to reverse the implications of the epigraph, to show that, in his version of prehistory, the 'monsters' with 'cunning brains . . . and possibly cannibalistic tendencies' are not the Neanderthals but the evolutionary subsequent *homo sapiens*. In framing most of the novel from the point of view of one of the Neanderthals, Lok, Golding tries carefully to duplicate the primitive perspective. The 'shambling gait', for example, is visible on the first page, when Lok is carrying the child, Liku, on his shoulders: 'His feet stabbed, he swerved and slowed.' At other times, he talks of his feet as 'no longer clever', or Golding adds that Lok's following the actions of others in his group is 'affectionate and unconscious parody'. The Neanderthals also flare nostrils grossly and are inhibited by their hairiness. They do not discriminate perceptions sharply and rationally, thinking in a kind of amalgamated metaphor as in describing 'lumps of smooth grey rock' as 'the bones of the land' (Chapter I). This perspective makes the Neanderthals appealing, although Golding could hardly do everything necessary to characterise them through their own eyes. Frequently, he breaks apart from the Neanderthal perspective to add an authorial voice. When Lok, having been hungry and eaten meat, is satisifed and 'became Lok's belly', Golding adds that 'his face shone with grease and serene happiness'. In the next sentence, Golding goes further to show what that is generally human Lok could not do: 'Tonight was colder than last night, though he made no comparisons' (Chapter IV). Occasionally, the authorial intrusions become more abstract, as in the confusion Lok shares with Fa, a female member of the group, when they first see a human being and Golding explains that 'There was nothing in life as a point of reference' (Chapter V).

Despite these probably necessary intrusions that interrupt the Neanderthal's point of view and despite what may be oversimplification of Wells, Golding does build a coherent, appealing and effective fictional portrait of the earlier species. The Neanderthals, or 'people', as they refer to themselves, are made amiable and attractive. Despite their perceptual limitations, the ingeniously conveyed strictures placed on their rational intelligence, the 'people' are warm and responsive. They have a deep and humble sense of their own limitations, as well as a faith in a female divine power (whom they call 'Oa') and in the goodness of the earth. Although we see a group of only eight 'people' (and one of these is a child, another an infant), they enjoy a family life free from fighting, guilt and emotional squabbling. Each has his or her function, carefully defined and limited, each a respect for the other members of the family. Their values are communal rather than individual, for they have no sense of private ownership or sole emotional claim. They all warm the Old Man with their bodies as he is dying. Their sexuality is also communal, for, although Lok and Fa sometimes seem to be mates, Liku is the daughter of Lok and Nil. Nil is the child-bearing woman and Ha the most intelligent man, although the four share sexual relationships, work and spontaneous concern and appreciation for the others. Their emotions centre on what is fundamental: food, shelter and closeness; birth, life and death. They keep and protect the image of Oa, the goddess that the Old Man tells them 'brought forth the earth from her belly. . . . The earth brought forth woman and the woman brought forth the first man out of her belly.' They share a vision of a previous paradise, unlike the colder and more difficult present, a time 'when there had been many people, the story that they all liked so much of the time when it was summer all year round and the flowers and fruit hung on the same branch.' They also have a strongly developed moral sense, not only toward each other but also toward other beings on the earth. When, at one point, out foraging for food, Lok and Fa bring back a deer, Fa assures him that 'A cat has killed the deer and sucked its blood, so there is no blame' (Chapter II).

The 'people' are, however, severely limited in conceptualising themselves. They sometimes split themselves literally into an inside and an outside, as if the two have no connection. Their conceptions of the exterior world are similarly blurred. On their annual migration with which the novel begins, they notice that a log they use to cross a deep stream is no longer there and they assume it has gone away. When the log they find to try to replace it does not hold, they assume the log swims as they assume the sun hides itself. They carry their fire with them, reverently, as if, like Prometheus, they had taken it from the

Gods. Their fire is transported as a smouldering spark surrounded by wet clay that they open, blow to flame and feed. Although the fire seems to suit both their needs and their devotion to exterior power, they generally have little capacity as incipient engineers or organisers of the exterior world to maintain themselves. In the middle of a process that requires several consecutive steps, like building a bridge, they sometimes forget the first step before they have finished the second. Some, like Fa, are brighter than others, like Lok, in maintaining consecutive memory and in connecting cause and effect rationally. For all of them, however, language is a commitment that establishes unchangeable reality. Once something is spoken, it *is*, even when the words are those of the dying, hallucinatory Old Man who never recovers from the chill he caught by falling in the water during their inept attempt to reconstruct a bridge to replace the missing log. Imagination is not conveyed by speech; rather their imagination takes the form of 'pictures', images of the world that they dimly apprehend and try to sort out. When something happens outside their comprehension, they recognise that they have 'no pictures' and, therefore, no imagination, memory or words. They try, honestly and literally, to construct their world from those 'pictures' that they do observe and remember, and then to solidify, make permanent, that world through language.

Golding is most effective in describing the process, the way the minds of the 'people' try to sort out the 'pictures' of a changing exterior world. The 'people' are invariably direct, working out their perceptions honestly as far as they can (although they are capable of a warm humour, regarding Lok as the buffoon of the group when he nonsensically uses words for which he has no 'pictures'). Golding combines the moral respect and sympathy with the insistence on the intellectual limitation, the problems in connecting cause with effect or the difficulty in summoning a 'picture' and converting it into usable experience like speech. At times, Golding shows this process operating through a long scene, as in the one in which Lok and Fa fight off the hyenas and buzzards for the prize of the doe the cat has killed. Although Fa dimly understands, as Lok does not, that the feared cat will not return to a kill whose blood has been drained, she cannot convert her understanding into speech, although she can express the moral issue in asserting that there is no blame. The passage works in its compressed complexity, in the sense that understanding differently, intellectually or rationally separate although emotionally and morally congruent, one creature fearful, the other not, the two can work together to bring food home to the family. Golding creates a striking *tour de force*, a condensed prose metaphor that uses the 'people', with all their adequacies and inadequacies, to illustrate the qualities that he sees as simultaneously prior and fundamental to what we are able to regard only as human experience. The accuracy of Golding's version of Wells is irrelevant; we convert the moral and emotional implications of the metaphor into a statement about primal or basic human nature.

The Inheritors, however, does not rest in its metaphor of the mind of the 'people', as its action is not confined to the stasis of their decline and evolutionary replacement by *homo sapiens*. Rather, Golding introduces the new species, the human being, at first just as seen from the point of view of the 'people', then, in the short final chapter, with a switch to the human point of view. Human society is full of noise, fights and anger, of provocation, infidelity and betrayal. The individual, understanding and projecting more of his or her imagination, is capable of setting self against community, of trying to gain power or love at the expense of a fellow being. Lok and Fa, looking at the human beings from a distance, can see that they are predatory, that they have 'teeth that remembered wolf'. Lok and Fa are far from able to understand much that they see, although Fa is able to state the moral comment 'Oa did not bring them out of her belly' (Chapter IX). Only gradually is Lok able to realise that the long stick he sees from a distance that the human being holds is a bow and the tiny cross-stick that whizzes past his head into a tree is an arrow meant to harm him. He takes even longer to recognise that the human beings have captured Liku; when he does realise this, he thinks they wanted her only as a playmate for one of their children approximately her own age. He tries, at first, to throw food for her. The human beings, however, turn Liku into food, killing her in a ritual sacrifice when their hunt is a failure and devouring her remains. Worship is not respect or devotion but predatory propitiation. Liku, like Simon in *Lord of the Flies* (also like 'you', human beings generically), is the scapegoat, the sacrificial victim to predatory human evil. The 'people' will eat meat only when it is already dead, drained, and they can absolve themselves of 'blame'; human beings, more technologically skilful and rationally intelligent, will eat what they kill no matter how close the species is to themselves. The more intelligently individual and the more accurately self-conscious, the crueller and more evil the species. The 'people' had difficulty in separating themselves from the exterior world; the human being as a post-lapserian creature, more intelligently divided, more conscious of what the individual self is, makes martyrs and victims out of his own species.

The moral and intellectual contrast between the 'people' and the human beings is not Golding's final statement in *The Inheritors*, for both species are capable of some amount of significant change through experience. The novel is about evolution, not only from one species to another, but of the capacities within each of the species themselves. Golding displays two senses of movement within the novel: from one species to the next; in a quicker, more impacted and interior way, from lesser to greater consciousness within each species. The final chapter shifts to the point of view of Tuami, one of the human beings. Although still the evil and individualistic human being, he is able to abandon his plot to kill his chief, recognising that the single action of his knife-blade would, at best, be only a sharp point against the overwhelming darkness of the world he would also exemplify. He can feel guilt and 'grief'; he can also recognise the possibilities of love and light. In short, Tuami's consciousness has expanded from a representation of man's essential evil to the suggestion of a more complex representation of fallible human possibility. Tuami, in the log he has made into a boat, ends the novel by looking at the light flashing on the water and 'he could not see if the line of darkness had an ending'. Toward the end of the novel, Lok also learns as he observes the human beings and tries to create 'pictures' of what they are. He begins to imagine similes, and, as Golding comments directly, 'Lok discovered "Like",' which he had 'used . . . all his life without being aware of it'. Through his elementary understanding of simile, Lok begins to establish a prior condition for sorting out individuality, for understanding how creatures are both like and unlike each other. One of his similes seems crucially symbolic: 'They are like the river and the fall, they are a people of the fall; nothing stands against them' (Chapter X). In the final chapter, Tuami watches as Fa (always a few steps ahead of Lok) is precipitated over the falls to her death, a process the now diminished Lok, seen from a distance, is sure to follow. In the process of evolution, Golding symbolically suggests, the Neanderthals have fallen into humanity and attention shifts to the already explicitly human creature who can experience guilt and self-knowledge, just as he can adapt and master the log (suggestions of the 'Tree of Knowledge'), which defeated the 'people' in the initial episode of the novel. The fall into humanity is both a lost innocence and a 'fortunate' fall, fortunate in its recognition of human consciousness and the possibility, however dim, of redemption. The questions of likeness and difference, of one species against the other, have been transformed into a powerfully searching and traditionally religious statement about the nature of the human being.

As Golding's metaphorical statement deepens, the epigraph from Wells seems more a prod than an alternative, a propellant to the fictional explosion. Initially a response to what Golding regards as erroneous simplification in Wells's *Outline of History*, just as *Lord of the Flies* was a response to the confidence in civilisation in Ballantyne's fiction, *The Inheritors* becomes a more dense and searching statement about the human condition than any scientifically documentable polarity between Neanderthal and *homo sapiens* might suggest. Golding's account of evolution is simultaneously physical, rational, moral and religious, all conveyed in compact statements of similarity and difference in language that is both concrete and strikingly resonant, explosive prose. A description as 'fable' accounts for *The Inheritors* even less than it does for *Lord of the Flies*, for the pattern of matching action or the progress of narrative to meaning would imply a more simplified and linear process of evolution than that which Golding represents in the novel. The form of the 'fable', in its insistence on the significance of action, would restrict Golding's treatment of the human condition. Nor can one designate *The Inheritors* as 'myth' really achieved, for 'myth', at least in so far as one understands the Classical and Christian myths that echo so strongly through Golding's consciousness, requires an application to and assent from the general literature culture that is difficult to demonstrate in contemporary terms. Perhaps some future age will see Golding's original works as establishing 'myth' with twentieth-century referents (perhaps 'myth', on this level, can only be seen or applied retrospectively), but his powerful fiction seems too individual and idiosyncratic a version of the traditional to operate as the kind of 'myth' to which the literate culture assents. Rather, escaping from both the boundaries suggested by the form of 'fable' and the lines suggested by simple response to the prods and or propellants, the Ballantyne and the Wells, *Lord of the Flies* and *The Inheritors* evolve into distinctive and unique fictions. Without the propellants to set them in action, they might seem incoherent or mysterious, certainly difficult, and the simplified polarity is probably the best point of entrance into Golding's fictional world. But his own kind of form, his own incorporation of literary and religious tradition into an essential statement of the human conditon, is not really achieved until his next novel, his next unique and symbolic literary explosion.

[handwritten margin notes:] Contrast in culture

characters Lok

Fa

Tuami

Liku

what g is trying to say

setting

4

The Metaphor: *Pincher Martin, Free Fall* and *The Spire*

Those who regarded Golding's first two novels as fully explained by the form of the fable were puzzled and intrigued at the appearance of *Pincher Martin* in 1956. Although the novel seems to be the story of a war-time sailor whose ship has been torpedoed, clinging to a rock in the cold North Atlantic in an effort to survive, we learn conclusively at the end, when his body is washed ashore, that he died at the beginning of the novel. He had never had time to kick off his boots as Golding describes him as doing before climbing on to the rock on the fourth page. Golding's treatment removes the dimension of time, focuses attention on the depiction of man in a timeless, universal state. The form of fable, in which narrative progress suggests the author's values by a consecutive account of what has happened, a linear chain that conveys a version of what causes what, can provide no satisfactory explanation for a narrative that does not involve time, progress and causation. Even long before the recognition that the sailor, Christopher Martin, called 'Pincher', the standard nickname for Martins in the Royal Navy (here the Christ-bearer turned into the character who appropriates what belongs to others for himself), has been dead all along, Golding provides numerous indications that the novel is not a linear struggle for survival. Besides the name, Pincher is a symbolic man, isolated in timeless symbolic space – 'everywhere the darkness was grainless and alike. There was no wreckage, no sinking hull, no struggling survivors but himself, there was only darkness lying close against the balls of his eyes' (Chapter I). In addition, the possibilities for rescue are undercut from the very beginning of the novel. Shapes cannot be ships, from Pincher's human point of view, and the shadows of size and distance that might permit one to anticipate or imagine rescue are made far too vague to function in terms of any human consciousness.

The disappearance of the usual human conceptions of time and space force the attention to another realm, that of Pincher as metaphor for the pain and 'grief' of human experience. Pincher extends both microcosmically and macrocosmically: he 'pictures' a little jam jar in which 'one could see into a little world . . . which was quite separate but which one could control', a jar with a 'little glass figure . . . delicately balanced between opposing forces'; he also sees himself as the figure in the jam jar, in 'dangerous stability, poised between floating and going down' by his 'lifebelt'. He recognises his suspension, his body that breathes apart from his mind and his imagination that recognises the pain of its partial and insufficient control. He 'could not use the mechanism for regular breathing but it took air in gulps between the moments of burial' (Chapter I). The metaphor is reminiscent of all those painfully graphic divisions of soul and body, of the human being wracked by the pains of the divided self, the opposed qualities incongruous and inseparable, that characterise a good deal of the seventeenth-century metaphysical poetry that Golding had earlier claimed he rejected. The human position is conveyed with startling force as the figure is suspended between his desires and his incapacities, his nature as Christ-bearer and as Pincher, his soul and his body.

In the second chapter, Golding extends the metaphor to the terrain on which most of the novel takes place. Martin finds a rock, an imagined solidity as against the constantly moving and solvent water in which he is immersed. But the rock is also human pain – human salvation and human torture simultaneously. The pain is the anguish of an aching tooth, as Golding calls the rock the 'peak of a mountain range, one tooth set in the ancient jaw of a sunken world, projecting through the inconceivable vastness of the whole ocean' (Chapter II). As Martin climbs the rock, attempting to use it as the locus of his survival and salvation, the rock is lashed by destructive, sometimes overwhelming, tides. Yet he notices that limpets can survive by clinging to the sides of the rock. Both limpet and tooth, both tiny creatures struggling to survive and repository of all localised human pain, Martin clings to his rock. He clings

to a vision of survival, a tangible and craggy mind, in the midst
of the raging waters of the body. Golding's metaphor for human
experience, soul and body, is conveyed with tangible and
impacted force.

Locking his subject into the duality of these Christian
metaphysical positions, of body and soul, Golding connects his
Christopher who is a Pincher to the lonely and painfully
exposed rock. Pincher is a castaway, a man isolated from
community in all the agonised essence of his divided being. He
is set within constant shattering cold, hunger and storms, the
sufferings of human experience. Golding dramatises the most
acute suffering in terms of physical pain, with frequent passages
like 'The pain in the corner of his eye went with him too. This
was the most important of all the pains because it thrust a
needle now into the dark skull where he lived. The pain could
not be avoided. His body revolved around it' (Chapter III).
The pain is also a spur, goading Martin to use his human
rationality and skill to try to survive on the rock.

In so far as the narrative is linear at all, most of the story of
Martin on the rock is the story of his conscious human effort to
survive. Martin is the rationalist, the Cartesian, equating his
identity with his capacity to think, to work out consciously
what he can do to survive and encourage rescue. He names
parts of the rock, for example, 'the High Street', 'the Red Lion',
'the Dwarf', and 'Food Cliff', to impose logical and familiar
geography in an attempt to control his experience. The
geography becomes the structure for the periodic routine of
finding what minimal food and shelter he can: 'If this rock tries
to adapt me to its ways I will refuse and adapt it to mine. I will
impose my routine on it, my geography' (Chapter VI). But his
geography is not the measure of the rock itself, as Golding
keeps shifting the dimensions outside of human control.
Sometimes the crevices seem habitable shelters within the rock,
namable and bounded; at other times, the crevices become
larger than the rock, subsume it in emptiness. Pincher fears
illness and madness, whatever will deprive him of the capacity
to calculate carefully his possible means of survival. And,
although he has no staff or stick, no obvious property that
might signal his existence to an outside world, he constantly
thinks about and plots possible rescue. He gathers seaweed,
laboriously ascends 'Look-out', and, in an elaborately described

process of engineering, arranges the seaweed, vertically and horizontally, in the shape of a cross. He uses the seaweed 'to impose an unnatural pattern on nature, a pattern that would cry out to any rational beholder – Look! Here is thought. Here is man!' Rescue and Christian salvation are equated, as he envisions that 'the rock will become a hot cross bun' (Chapter VIII). Martin thinks he may be able to plot or earn, to control, his salvation. In one of his confident moments, he cries out at the raging and uncontrollable sea: 'I don't claim to be a hero. But I've got health and education and intelligence. I'll beat you' (Chapter V). This passage and others underline the egotism involved in Martin's attempt to claim salvation through his own rational efforts. Rationalism, for Golding, is arrogant and presumptive, the human being's delusion that his thought and consciousness can name and master the conditions of the universe. In continuing to struggle on the assumption that he can create his salvation, Pincher gives to human effort a universally unwarranted authority that is itself his damnation.

Once the metaphor is established as a statement of essential humanity on the isolated rock, Golding begins to give Pincher a particular past that can be realised, through flash-backs, in individual and social terms. Pincher has been a creature of the modern, cosmopolitan world, naming parts of his rock, for example, 'Oxford Circus, Piccadilly and Leicester Square' (Chapter VI). His whole life is gradually reflected inside his aching head in 'pictures', the same term that Golding used in *The Inheritors* for perceptions and points of experience recalled for which the creature has no controlling and formulatable concepts, no language. Pincher creates words for his 'pictures' and exults in his mastery. But the 'pictures' are not completely expressed by the self-justifying language and they remain alternately burning and freezing, or sometimes stabbing, his head with sins and guilts. As a 'Pincher', Martin has always taken what had belonged to others, justifying his actions in terms of his desire to survive as well as he could, his rational skill and his intelligence. He has acted out his rational capacity, although he has been only an actor, professionally and personally, having no identity other than those he has simulated in a succession of roles. He is like the vaguely existential protagonists, in the fiction of Golding's contemporaries, who know themselves only through the roles they play. But Pincher is seen from a morally different point of view. As his 'pictures' of his past keep recurring, we recognise that he has slept with his producer's wife to advance his career, been responsible for serious injury to a friend by driving his motorcycle egotistically and dangerously, and betrayed both males and females close to him. He has even enjoyed the pain he caused others, maliciously leading a friend to Pincher's own bedroom to discover the woman the friend loves, Pincher thus betraying both the woman with whom he is having an affair and his male friend. Enjoying most his role in a morality play that dramatised the seven deadly sins, Pincher has always just taken the best of anything he has just happened to want, and 'greed' is the sin the other actors finally decide describes him most accurately. In the principal morality play of his own life, Pincher has twice betrayed his best friend, the 'saint', Nathaniel. He raped Nathaniel's wife, after serving as 'best man' at their wedding ceremony; on the ship in the North Atlantic, while on the bridge at the crucial moment, Pincher gave the order to turn hard starboard (which would have been right for avoiding the fatal torpedo had it been given a few moments earlier) as a kind of reflex action to shake Nathaniel, who was leaning at the rail praying, off the ship. Nathaniel is Pincher's goad, his conscience, always warning him. Pincher needs to shake him off, betray him, even consciously and casually consider murdering him, in order to preserve his own sinful ego, the complete autonomy of his greedy, rationalist, thinking, human self.

We never know whether or not Nathaniel, Golding's example of the man who can abandon ego, his 'saint', is ultimately saved. The novel follows and records Pincher, and he is damned. His rational and conscious efforts cannot save him; his insistence on self, the insistence on his relentless attempts to get whatever he can to comfort or assuage his ego, his 'greed', ensures his moral damnation in a universe not controlled by man. As Golding has said a number of times, Pincher himself *is* purgatory.[35] The metaphor is the novel, a novel constantly propelled toward a centre of human experience. When Pincher is trying to collect his conscious strengths to focus on survival, he recognises: 'There was at the centre of all the pictures and pains and voices a fact like a bar of steel, a thing – that which was so nakedly the centre of everything that it could not even examine itself. In the darkness of the skull, it existed, a darker dark, self-existent and indestructible' (Chapter III). The darkness is within his own body. He sometimes thinks of himself as Atlas or as Prometheus, but the darkness is insistently there, the patterns he imposes on experience are 'unnatural', and his hands, his tools, for example, are seen as intrinsically lobster claws, as pinchers. Toward the end of the novel, just before the raging water sweeps him away from the rock, his body later, in the coda to the novel, to be discovered washed ashore and he having died instantaneously, Pincher, the timeless human purgatory, is unrepentant. Perceiving 'branches of black lightning' as something outside himself with extraordinary power, Pincher has no words, 'no mouth'. He cannot consciously respond, but the fear and the rage at his centre 'screamed into the pit of nothing voicelessly, wordlessly. "I shit on your heaven!"' (Chapter XIII). Martin's 'Christ-bearing' is completely inverted and the only possible salvation, left shadowy and undramatised, is perhaps reserved for Nathaniel. Within the novel, Golding dramatises human evil, the sense of original sin, with stark power, his metaphors echoing along the lines of physical apprehension. The physicality gives the metaphorical concept intensity. Intensity is also conveyed through another version of Pincher's 'greed', his often reiterated determination to have what he wants 'at all costs'. The phrase, which is even more central to Golding's next novel, *Free Fall*, underlines the total selfishness and greed of the creature who thinks his consciousness and satisfaction the single measure of all humanity. The intensity of the conception is itself Golding's moral judgement.

The same version of the nature of the human being is carried over into Golding's next two novels, *Free Fall* and *The Spire*, although the metaphor is extended in time in one novel and through space in the other. *Free Fall* extends the central conception of human sin through the course of an individual life, the time of Sammy Mountjoy. Instead of creating the focus on the nature of the creature, the being, as in *Pincher Martin*, Golding in *Free Fall* concentrates on how a similar character came to reveal his sinful nature, on the process of becoming. In tracing the process, Golding constantly examines moral questions, locates which actions can be judged and which cannot, so that the novel radiates a much more severe sense of moral judgement than does *Pincher Martin*, although the moral implications are identical. In *Free Fall*, narrated in the first person by the artist, Sammy Mountjoy, Golding begins by having Sammy retrospectively ask himself to locate the moment at which he lost his freedom. The loss of free will, the beginning of the process of acting out the representations of the determined being, is the moment at which, in Golding's theological terms, Sammy can be held responsible for his actions, can be judged for abandoning freedom and control to live out some terrifyingly selfish inner human necessity. As Sammy says, 'I am looking for the beginning of responsibility, the beginning of darkness, the point where I began' (Chapter II).

In one sense, *Free Fall* follows a more conventional novelistic pattern than do Golding's earlier novels. When the novel first appeared, its unexpected gestures toward a more conventional framework than Golding's earlier novels pleased some readers and antagonised others. Sammy seems a more socially locatable representative of contemporary man, as his life chronicles the development of the artist amidst social circumstances that parallel those of the previous forty or fifty years of public history. Sammy is the artist who rejects all systems in his effort to understand himself and his world: 'I have hung all systems on the wall like a row of useless hats. They do not fit' (Chapter I). He traces his life through his individuality and his society. He recalls his childhood, his large, mild, feckless mother, the absence of a father, and his growing up in the slums of Rotten Row. He reflects his generation's scepticism, as the Second World War is about to begin, concerning the dogmas and political absolutes of either the left or the right. He recounts, in considerable detail, the influence of two teachers, whom he calls 'my parents not in the flesh' (Chapter XIV). One is Rowena Pringle, religious, dogmatic, unsympathetic and imaginative, telling, in false and snobbishly exclusive terms, the possibly true legendary stories of man's creation. The other is the kind scientist and rationalist, Nick Shales, refusing to believe what he cannot demonstrate in terms of physical fact. Golding, recognising that, in the process of education, 'people are the walls of our room, not philosophies', has Sammy follow Nick for a long time before realising that Rowena Pringle better understood human nature in a world in which it is human presumption to think that good and evil can be decided by majority vote.

Although these elements of background and education, like Sammy's later career as an artist and his imprisonment in a German camp during the Second World War, give the novel a strong sense of social specification, they also contain elements symbolically recognisable from Golding's earlier novels. As an artist, and he has been a putative artist since early childhood, Sammy both thinks and imagines in 'pictures', in graphic representations of what he is that he cannot express in words. His process of becoming an artist is that of learning to refine and develop his skill with his 'pictures', also to accommodate them to 'pictures' that others will recognise and applaud, a process that does not necessarily yield the understanding of sin, human nature, freedom and responsibility on which the novel focuses. Unlike the process in many conventional novels about the growth of the artist, the artistic process itself, in Golding's terms, is not a metaphor for coming to understand human nature. The artist and his understandable world are, in some sense, repellent to Golding, immoral, representing a process more likely to obscure understanding than to encourage it. Sammy's surrogate parents are also represented as an extreme version of the innately human polarity visible in Golding's earlier fiction as illustrating the two alternate means for controlling or understanding experience, the contradictory ways of life of the religious and the rational. As Sammy concludes, when reflecting on them at the end of the novel, on Rowena Pringle's continuing vitality in retirement and on Nick Shales' heart attack: 'Her world was real, both worlds are real. There is no bridge' (Chapter XIV). The polarity, the co-existence of body and soul intrinsic to human nature, cannot be reconciled by human beings.

The compression of the issues of the novel into drama does not depend on an attempt to reconcile body and soul. Rather, the narration dramatically focuses on Sammy's attempt to isolate the point of change in himself, to find the moment at which he lost the innocence of freedom and chose to express his inner nature. To some extent, in terms of the novel's focus and resolution, the issue of body and soul is a false one, for, in the process of ransacking his past and returning to his schooldays, Sammy keeps 'picturing' the alternate and irreconcilable worlds of religion and the rational as his memory moves from the

universe of one classroom to the entirely different universe of
the other. Yet he realises that 'Miss Pringle vitiated her
teaching. She failed to convince, not by what she said but by
what she was. Nick persuaded me to his natural scientific
universe by what he was not by what he said' (Chapter XI).
This conflict, through its essentially human nature, is permanent
and unbridgeable, and so finally falsely dramatic in that drama
suggests the possibility of resolving an issue through time. Since
Golding spends considerable narrative time dealing with the
locked conflict between religion and reason that goes back and
forth in a dramatic structure without relevation, many readers
find the novel less intense and interesting than *Pincher Martin* or
The Spire. Yet the novel is given intense and dramatic focus
through a theme visible from Sammy's schooldays. This is his
artist's fascination with and pursuit of Beatrice Ifor, the vision
of love that suggests Dante's unattainable Beatrice. Critics have
variously explained her last name as 'if-or', expressing Beatrice's
uncertainty and equivocation, or as 'I-for', more plausibly and
centrally shifting attention to Sammy's ruthlessly single-minded
pursuit of her.

The novel connects Sammy's pursuit with his art, for the first
incident he recalls is his accidentally perfect schoolboy drawing
of Beatrice that he allowed a friend who could not draw to
claim for his own. Sammy is then obsessed with the desire to
draw Beatrice perfectly again, but he cannot duplicate his
accidental success. Yet this, in itself, is not the moment Golding
localises for Sammy's loss of freedom. The artistic impulse,
although egotistical and a removal from or a deflection of what
Golding regards as central human experience, is not the issue
on which crucial judgement of the human being depends. Nor
are earlier instances of Sammy's victimisation, like his
undeserved beating by a verger, for evil is not explicable simply
as a response to evil received from others. Golding carefully
tracks the course of the entire relationship between Sammy and
Beatrice: his various schoolboy ploys to gain her attention; his
insistence on making love to her, despite her initial equivocation
that seems much closer to indifference; her sacrificial submission
to her sexuality; their marriage and Sammy's exploitation of
her for his career in that his paintings of her bring him his first
artistic success; his infidelity with Taffy, the sexually liberated
and pleasure-loving daughter of a Communist. Sammy concludes

each of these episodes with the statement that he could not here locate his fall, his loss of innocence and freedom, for the fall was already determined. Yet he continues to feel guilt, to try to locate the point of responsibility. Beatrice has never been anything other than passive, constantly victimised by Sammy, her life destroyed by his claiming her and then abandoning her. After the Second World War, when he last sees her, she is a patient in a mental hospital, unable to relate to others or control her experience at all. When Sammy visits, she, in the anxiety that is her only sign of life, is unable even to control her bladder and urinates on the floor. Just before this symbolic episode, Sammy, in one of his frequent reflections on his own past that constitute the structure of flash-backs on which the novel is built, has finally located the origin of his guilt and his loss of freedom. After recalling again the schoolboy incident of his drawing and his failure to duplicate it, he recalled another half-forgotten incident when, talking with a friend, he resolved to do anything he could to claim Beatrice's attention. The friend objected that she was indifferent to him, thought him depraved, even disliked him. Sammy replied that 'If I want something enough I can always get it provided I am willing to make the appropriate sacrifice', which is 'everything' (Chapter XII). For Golding, that single-mindedness, relentless insistence on self, and exclusion of the rest of the universe in order to satisfy the imposing demands of the ego, is the definition of original sin. And Sammy's location of the sin in time, in the course of his life, completes his understanding of the guilt he cannot expunge, the fallen nature he cannot change.

In Golding's terms, the human being is intrinsically a microcosmic image of the greater forces of the universe. Frequent images suggest both the diversity and the connections of human experience: 'Oh, the continent of a man, the peninsulas, capes, deep bays, jungles and grasslands, the deserts, the lakes, the mountains and high hills!' (Chapter X). Sammy's attempts to defend himself on existential grounds – 'For, after all, in this bounded universe, I said, where nothing is certain but my own existence' or 'Nothing was permanent, nothing was more than relative. Sex was a private business' (Chapter VI) – are seen as self-deceptive attempts to deny human nature and sanctify the changes in time and the individual self. When Sammy sees Beatrice incurably ill at the end of the novel, he asks the doctor (himself implicated in human guilt since he is interested in Sammy's current wife, Taffy) if he, Sammy, can be held responsible. The doctor equivocates, saying that Sammy might or might not have 'tipped' the balance of her sanity, might have been the principal cause or might possibly have delayed what was bound to emerge anyhow. In particular terms of cause and effect, within particular fragments of time, guilt cannot easily be assigned. But, in the larger sense, in the sense of violating appropriate human connections, of an ego dedicating itself to the impingement on another, to the satisfaction of self, Sammy is clearly guilty, another of Golding's examples of fallen man, man who was 'free' to fall or not fall and chose to express his sinful ego.

Sammy has also been the victim of other egos. During the Second World War, he was captured by the Nazis and held in a German prison camp. His interrogation that became a torture was another's evil imposition on him, conducted by an inquisitor named Dr Halde ('halde' is the German word for 'slope', suggesting a downward vector or descent). Fortunately and unpredictably, Sammy is released from the inquisition, not because of either his courage or his cowardice, which are equivocal anyhow, but rather because the commandant inexplicably decides not to pursue the illegal torturing process longer. Recalled in the final line of the novel, the commandant tells Sammy that Halde 'does not know about peoples'. The implications of the statement suggest that the consequences of egotistic imposition are not always certain or predictable. But the nature of imposition is always immoral and inhumane. The imposition of the ego, the sacrifice of everything to itself, the deliberate human appropriation of experience to itself and its satisfactions, its body, *is* evil, for it violates a sense of human community and connection, a sense of the world larger than the individual. The human being is both isolated and connected to others, just as he is both rational and spiritual, both body and mind. And between the isolated ego and the more fully sentient apprehension of others or community, just as between the selfish body and the more imaginative mind, Golding, in this novel, keeps insisting that 'There is no bridge'. *Free Fall* provides no 'bridge' and resolves no human dilemmas. Rather, the novel traces the process through time of one social and historical man becoming representative of contemporary manifestations of evil.

Golding's next novel, *The Spire*, extends the central metaphor of body and soul in spatial terms through the visible and public form of architecture. *The Spire* is the story of the construction of the largest tower in England, built on to the already existent structure of the cathedral. The metaphor constantly encapsulates both the acclivity of constructing the tower and the declivity and degradation of exposing the pit of slime on which the foundations of the cathedral rest. The fictional cathedral is obviously modelled on the cathedral at Salisbury, the one to which the largest tower in England was added 100 years after the original construction. Golding's essay, 'An Affection for Cathedrals', published a year after the novel, indicates that he had Salisbury, with which he had long been familiar, in mind when writing the novel. In Golding's version, problems of constructing a spire are manifest, for apart from the theory that to balance forces a structure must extend as far below the earth as it extends above, no plans for attaching a spire to the original foundations excavated for the cathedral exist. Four hundred feet of masonry need to be extended into the air; four hundred feet need to be propped, controlled, down in the slime beneath. In both the novel and history, many have believed the construction of the spire at Salisbury impossible. Even as recently as 1899, a well-known Victorian architect regarded the original builders of the cathedral as wantonly careless and thought adding the spire a 'foolhardy enterprise'.[36]

The novel returns to the metaphorical mode of *Pincher Martin*, using the central figure as the metaphor, seen with detachment, rather than tracing the process of developing the metaphor through a particular consciousness, as in *Free Fall*. Jocelin, the dean of the cathedral, determined to build the spire, is the central figure seen from a third person point of view. He is himself a reflection of the architectural metaphor, depicted as lying on his 'back in the marshes, crucified, and his arms were transepts', while he feels himself both sinking in the pit and holding his eyes fixed on the sky (Chapter III). Part of Jocelin's motive is truly devotional, 'the important level of light . . . a true dimension' (Chapter I); part of his motive is also individual and a form of repressed sexuality, an ascending achievement that both imposes and establishes himself. Anxious to achieve the spire, obsessed with seeing it built before he dies, Jocelin is also aware of his depths, the stink of the pit that represents his own decay and twisted sexuality, all that he has buried within himself. The novel's dense, impacted, resonant prose reflects the intensity and the divisions within Jocelin. In addition, the progress of the narrative, not following that of consecutive time or that of the conscious attempt to locate experience in *Free Fall*, resembles that of *Pincher Martin*, proceeding through successive revelations of Jocelin's sin and guilt, his depths, that match the progressive acclivity of the spire that is finally built. Jocelin achieves self-knowledge, but not in any form he can use to transform his experience. He has built the spire, but is himself always both spire and pit.

Associates of Jocelin, other characters in the novel, are part of the same human nature and intimately connected to Jocelin, for the cathedral and spire are public and communal symbols. The builder is Roger Mason, a powerful and sceptical man who frequently doubts what he is doing and regards Jocelin as the Devil for establishing economic and sexual imperatives that keep Roger at the difficult task he does not welcome. Roger's affair with the attractive, red-haired Goody Pangall, encouraged by Jocelin, keeps him at work. Yet Jocelin eventually recognises that he himself has long desired Goody sexually, has, in fact, kept her near him at the cathedral by having arranged for her marriage to Pangall, the impotent caretaker who limps. Childless and full of contempt for her husband, Goody eagerly welcomes Roger, himself childless because his derisive wife, Rachel, has always laughed and mocked whenever they were together. Jocelin, watching from the outside, at first hardly recognising the sexuality and the emotions within himself, is vicariously part of the sexual drama. Pangall is murdered, either by Roger or by other workmen whom the bitter, self-pitying caretaker invariably annoys (the scene is described in such a way that one cannot tell, and Jocelin's viewpoint is blocked – but individual responsibility is not the issue anyhow), and is buried in the huge, charnel-like pit, rank with the decay of seepage from earlier graves, that Roger has used to demonstrate to Jocelin the folly of his undertaking. Pangall, who swept the cathedral with his broom of crossed staves, is the scapegoat, the impotent victim of all human activity – yet not the saintly or

revelatory scapegoat of Golding's earlier novels. Rachel discovers
her husband's infidelity with Goody Pangall. Her screams and
fury at Goody, who is pregnant by Roger, help bring on
Goody's miscarriage and death. She becomes another kind of
scapegoat. All Jocelin's complicity, his knowledge and
encouragement, his ineffectual or inefficient attempts to help,
and his bits and pieces of half self-knowledge ensure that he
shares the guilt for all the misery and disaster his project has
brought to the surface.

Within all the human mire and complexity, the tower gets
built. Golding is elaborately detailed in describing all the feats
of engineering involved, the construction and placement of
beams and cross-beams, the carving and heavy placement of
stone, and the various means designed to shore foundations and
forestall the creeping of the earth underneath. Often, the project
seems impossible. At one of the many points in the novel at
which he is anxious to abandon entirely or compromise the
height of the spire, Roger explains to Jocelin:

> We've nothing but a skin of glass and stone stretched between
> four stone rods, one at each corner. D'you understand that?
> The stone is no stronger than the glass between the verticals
> because every inch of the way I have to save weight, bartering
> strength for weight or weight for strength, guessing how
> much, how far, how little, how near, until my heart stops
> when I think of it. Look down, father. Don't look at me –
> look down! See how the columns at each corner are tacked
> together. I've clamped the stones together but still I can't
> make them stronger than stone. Stone snaps, crumbles, tears.
> Yet even now, when the pillars sing, perhaps this much may
> stand. I can give you a roof over it, and perhaps a weather
> vane that men will see for miles. (Chapter VI)

Jocelin bribes, preaches, religiously inspires and theocratically
forces him to continue building. At times, they think of the
spire as a miracle, the pillars 'floating'. Weather must also
constantly be assessed, used or forestalled depending on the
circumstances. Through searing heat, crippling cold and frost,
and a winter of rain so endless it changes permanently the
dimensions of the foundation pit already dug, the builder must
preserve his permeable materials. Through his prose and

references to Jocelin's confidence in what he doesn't understand, Golding tries to suggest that the medieval builders of the Salisbury spire, in the midst of similar problems and mysteries, did not recognise that the pits beneath the Salisbury marshes concealed an unusually strong weight-bearing geological formation.[37] With a system of engineering so new that many of the processes Roger invents and uses are unnamed, vague and only under partial control, the rising tower must be balanced against the shifting earth. The terms and perceptions are often imprecise, as they talk of pillars singing. The balance of forces, the acclivity and the depths, is only superficially a metaphor for Golding's familiar balances of faith and reason. Rather, the metaphor of the spatial position and lines of forces within the human creature extends in a number of more interesting and complex ways. Golding applies his balances of 'high' and 'low' to the theocratic structure that enables Jocelin to enforce his will, to the religious view of human nature that the dominant Christian symbol attempts to 'cross', and to sexual position and hierarchy that leaves the impotent Pangall the scapegoat in the pit, a position matched in the interior of Jocelin recognising the connection between the guilt of his repressions and the height of his aspirations. The spatial metaphor connects all of human experience, all its rare triumph and its frequent misery, 'the cost of building material' (Chapter VI).

More specifically than the symbol of the usual 'cross', the 'Holy Nail' represents the Christian coherence designed to keep the spire and the cathedral together. The Church in Rome had refused Jocelin's appeal for funds to build the spire, and he had, in one sense, compromised his project from the very beginning by welcoming funds from his Aunt Alison, a worldly former mistress of the King, who gave the money in return for Jocelin's promise to bury her in the cathedral. Rome offered the symbol of the 'Holy Nail' instead, the symbol of the price of human salvation, as Jocelin recalls the rhyme that 'For want of a nail the shoe was lost . . .' The 'Holy Nail' is delivered by an emissary from Rome and blessed; yet it also echoes the meaningless relic, bargained for or bought, and Aunt Alison regards it as a cheap trinket. Jocelin sees it as crucially significant, the way to make his spire, now finished and 'floating', secure, or in another image, the way to convert the spire of stone and glass into the natural aspiring force of his vision, 'a single green shoot at first, then clinging tendrils, then branches, then at last a riotous confusion' (Chapter IX). In the midst of a raging thunderstorm during the night after the 'Holy Nail' has been delivered and blessed, afraid the spire may topple, Jocelin feels he must place the nail on the spire himself, must demonstrate his faith in the human meaning of the spire. Although he suffers seriously from vertigo, he climbs the leaning and groaning spire himself. His spiritual climb is also compromised in that he keeps thinking of the dead Goody Pangall and his sexual attraction to her. He realises that she was the red-haired Satanic figure that troubled his dreams, as he realises fully, for the first time, his human connection to her in both guilt and sexual appeal. His vertigo is also his human self-recognition, and, despite the storm and the leaning tower, he hammers in the 'Holy Nail'. Back on the ground, he tells the still worldly and sceptical Aunt Alison, who thinks he has been a fool, that 'There's a level you can't understand' and that he has 'nailed' the spire 'to the sky' (Chapter X). The human being, in all his complexity, is connected to his universal meaning, and after the storm, the spire, although changed and leaning, still stands visible to all. The spire is, finally, the testament to faith that the 'Holy Nail' suggests, though 'Life itself is a rickety building'.

Sometime later, still not certain that the 'Holy Nail' will keep the spire from falling, Jocelyn attempts to expiate what he now sees as his sin in rejecting and 'killing' Goody Pangall. He calls on Roger Mason, now a drunk and muttering about his own guilts. When Jocelin confesses his guilt in Goody's death, Roger thinks that the Dean is accusing him, and no appropriate acknowledgement takes place in the storm of words between the two. Roger is so distressed at what he mistakenly sees as spiritual authority blaming him that he tries to commit suicide. Jocelin is left in his inexpungeable guilts, and in the illness that he has felt all along without ever being able to name it precisely. Golding now indicates that Jocelin has cancer of the spine, the metaphor for all the human corruption within the tense structure of his space. In a final scene, Jocelin lies dying looking out of his window at the spire that still stands. He sees it as a vision that 'had grown from some seed of rose-coloured substance that glittered like a waterfall, an upward waterfall'. He cannot name or sort out the spaces of his vision. Finally, in a moment of revelation before he dies, he finds a simpler metaphorical parallel and says that the spire is 'like the apple tree!' (Chapter

XII). He has always venerated the apple tree, the natural tree, aspiring in linear space and multiform simultaneously. The image of the tree keeps Jocelin suspended even in death. The spire is transformed into a symbol of natural man, and the apple tree suggests both the faith in aspiration and the inevitable fall from paradise.

In this, the phase of his most intense and concentrated fiction, Golding shaped extensive metaphors for humanity in a forceful version of traditional Christian concepts. He never articulated a 'bridge' to hold all he saw and thought into a theological consistency or a certain path through sin to redemption. His only 'bridge' was itself metaphorical and artistic, the power, intensity and depth of the coherent prose. The metaphors themselves, recalling Christian, Classical and other historical traditions, stated what he saw as permanently fallible and valuable about the nature of man, reaching with particular depth and intensity in those metaphors, tonally different from each other, that express and extend human nature spatially, *Pincher Martin* and *The Spire*. His language, especially in *The Spire*, often echoed the universal sonority of that in the seventeenth-century Biblical tradition. Golding no longer needed the somewhat artificial propellants of an antagonistic line of thought, the uses of Ballantyne and Wells in *Lord of the Flies* and *The Inheritors*, nor did he need the directed and restrictive plot line of the fable. Rather, the metaphors themselves became the novels. As metaphors, they left sufficient room for Golding's moral judgements about the contemporary world, as well as room for a deep and intense understanding of the inevitably fallible human creature. Metaphors may not have the cultural assent or authority of the myths that Golding hoped others might find that he wrote. But, in the diverse contemporary world, without being false to the complexity of that world, metaphor may be as close to myth as the serious and humanly fallible artist can come.

5

The Condition of England:
The Pyramid and *Darkness Visible*

Golding has always been a self-critical writer, as in his acknowledgement that his early fiction might be more concerned with ideas than with people. *The Pyramid*, published in 1967, can be read as his deliberate attempt to extend his range by using fiction to depict human character with more variety and particularity than he had before, or he might have wanted simply to try something else. The novel also apparently evolved differently from the others. Whereas the earlier novels like *The Inheritors* or *Pincher Martin* were single concepts which, although perhaps the product of a long period of gestation, were written with concentrated speed, *The Pyramid* seems to have been written in stages. Two of the novel's three parts appeared earlier in periodicals, the first part in *Kenyon Review*, the third part in *Esquire*. The focus on individualised characters and the less intensely singular method of construction create a novel without the severe dramatic and tragic intensity of the earlier fiction. *The Pyramid* presents man more as a semi-comic creature, able to choose and to learn, not locked in the potentially tragic dichotomies of his intrinsic nature. Whereas the other novels all depicted human experience at its extremity, at one or another penetrating version of its insolubility, *The Pyramid*, in the three episodes that trace the growth of Oliver's understanding, draws on a less metaphysical, more complex, perhaps more ordinary and familiar version of human experience.

All three episodes in the novel are related by Oliver in the first person, describing his complex relationships with others and what he learns from them. In the first episode, he is the sensitive young man of eighteen, 'a good time for suffering. One has all the necessary strength, and no defences.' The episode focuses on his relationship with the provocative Evie Babbacombe, the daughter of a retired sergeant who functions as the caretaker of the local Town Hall and the obsolete Town Crier. Oliver, teased and taunted by Evie, recognising both her attractions and the difference between her background and his anxious middle-class family (his father is a dispensing chemist, filling prescriptions for the town and dependent on the affluent doctor next door), slowly overcomes his inhibitions and begins a sexual relationship with Evie. Golding's prose matches the careful, complex, often comic evolution of Oliver's sexuality: 'She muttered, made some quick movements over her breasts with one hand. In our local complex of State Church, Nonconformity, and massive indifference, I had never seen anything like them.' Golding metaphorically establishes the sexuality as opposed to the local religious institutions, agents of repression – a very different process of fusing disparate elements of experience from the extreme, impacted, innate metaphors for human meaning that dominate the earlier novels.

In contrast to the affair between Sammy Mountjoy and Beatrice in *Free Fall*, in which Sammy's sexuality was the illustration of his ego that imposed and assaulted, the affair between Oliver and Evie is complex from its inception. After a series of secret meetings, they finally make love. Evie is both provocative and resistant, her moods alternating quickly; Oliver is both eager and frightened, powerfully attracted and shocked. She can be aggressive, delicate, warm-hearted and yielding; she is also promiscuous as she tells the fascinated and appalled Oliver of previous affairs in which she has offered herself for a variety of different reasons, conscious and unconscious. Against the inhibiting, hostile town, in terms of which she is seen as only a class representation, daughter of the seedy sergeant, sexuality is her only means of connection to others. Oliver, too, in coming to understand Evie, must defy his own background, the inhibitions and insistence on safety of his parents as well as the stereotyped social dimensions of his visionary aspirations. Oliver has won a scholarship to begin scientific studies at Oxford within a few months, and he has told himself that he is chastely in love with Imogen, the slightly older, elegant, aristocratic woman he hardly knows who is about to marry someone else. For both Evie and Oliver, as they come to understand themselves and each other a little better, sexuality is in defiance of the surrounding society, is an expression of the personal capacity to relate to other beings as against the stifling and isolating environment in which the human beings are set. Evie is banished from the town – not for her affair with Oliver, but as a result of the smudge of her lipstick on a young doctor's face – and Oliver goes to Oxford. At the end of the episode, when they meet accidentally a few years later, Oliver having sentimentalised the affair into just his sensitively orchestrated introduction to sexuality, Evie, after a few drinks, asserts that Oliver had raped her, that he understands little of cockroaches and rage, and that her father, the ostensibly quaint Town Crier and rigidly respectable sergeant, had introduced her to sex when she was a child. Oliver's understanding of both himself and his environment is still incomplete.

In posing the individual sexuality against the environment of the town, Golding is also both characterising the society and placing *The Pyramid* more within the conventions of the traditional nineteenth-century English novel than his earlier fiction had been. In the small town of 1930 that dominates the episode, Oliver fears that a kiss after midnight between teenagers is regarded as a moral flaw, almost as serious as a violation of caste. Oliver's family, when it notices them at all, patronises Evie's. Similarly, Oliver's family is patronised by the doctor's next door, and the boy of that family, Bobby Ewan, had regarded Oliver as his 'slave' when they played together as children. Oliver meets Evie through Bobby, Oliver still the 'slave' called late at night to borrow a car and rescue Evie and Bobby, out on an illicit date, from the quagmire into which Bobby had ineptly driven his father's car. Oliver's mother is a snob, viewing all relationships in terms of the social hierarchy, patronising or deferential to others as the social position indicates. Oliver's father is silent and inhibited, the remote scientist. After he, through his binolculars, accidentally sees Oliver and Evie making love on an exposed hillside outside of town, he explodes: '"There's – disease, you see. One's not suggesting that one's necessarily – been exposed to infection – but if one goes on like this" – for all his professed agnosticism the voice of generations of chapel burst out of him – "these books – cinema – papers – this sex – it's *wrong, wrong, wrong!*"'

When Oliver, in his frustration, thumps his piano so hard he smashes it (he is a musician as well as a scientist), his parents, in their grim concern, have the piano repaired and say not a word about it. Even during the short, most intense period of his relationship with Evie, Oliver cannot help thinking of his parents and their disapproval. He thinks of himself as dragging them down to 'where it was impossible to rise but always easy to fall – yes. I should kill them'. Class and the hypocrisies it engenders dominate all the local relationships. The town is appropriately called Stilbourne, not far from the larger town of Barchester, where they shop and where Imogen's wedding is to take place. The deliberate recall of both Salisbury and the world of Anthony Trollope is Golding's conscious placement of his concerns within the social dimensions of the nineteeth-century English novel. As John Fowles stated concerning a region slightly further south and west than Golding's (and, for Fowles, Hardy is the more constantly visible social progenitor than Golding's occasional Trollope), for this whole section of England the nineteenth century did not end until 1945.[38]

Golding has Oliver return to Stilbourne in 1963 for the setting of the third episode of *The Pyramid*. He notices the physical changes superimposed on the old outline: 'The familiar houses, bulged, leaned or slumped slightly out of true, had turned all Chelsea, with eggshell blue and one door of vivid yellow.' The town had 'been prettied, like some senile old lady, made presentable for visitors', and his father's cottage was now 'a visible piece of country quaintness, photogenic and sterile'. Stilbourne has not come to life. Underneath the chintz coverings, the town is only a tomb, physically and socially, that Oliver must disinter in order to reach his furthest point of understanding. But before he can approach this realisation, he must achieve something of the understanding he gains in the second episode, which takes place only a year after he has left Stilbourne for Oxford and includes Oliver's recognition of the hollow emptiness of his image of Imogen.

After his year of studying chemistry, Oliver returns and finds that his mother has enlisted him to fill a vacancy with a bit part playing the violin in a production of the Stilbourne Operatic Society. During the single rehearsal, Oliver notices more acutely now all the snobberies of the town, the lines of background and position that keep impeding the attempt at artistic production, despite the nominal control of a professional producer, Evelyn De Tracy, down from London. Oliver is at first excited by his proximity to Imogen and her husband, both cast in leading roles in the operetta, *The King of Hearts*, although he recognises that they are withdrawn and interested only in establishing their stage positions. When, in a stretch of free time during the production, having had to go outside and then get back in by another entrance (Golding develops effective comedy through the structure of amateur exits and entrances in the makeshift theatre of the Town Hall), Oliver stops in the pub next door, he unexpectedly encounters De Tracy. They have a drink together, and De Tracy, the representative of a wider artistic world, is sceptical and disconsolate about his experience in Stilbourne. He tells Oliver that, beneath the lacquer of her sweet smile, Imogen is a vain, stupid, insensitive woman without any talent at all. Her husband, as Oliver has already seen, is an oaf. As Oliver and De Tracy begin to talk of the sterile repressions of Stilbourne, and Oliver mentions his affair with Evie, the meeting on the hill 'practically in public', De Tracy shows Oliver some photographs of himself dressed in the costume of a ballerina. Innocent as he has been, Oliver learns in this episode that there are some forms of sexual liberation he would prefer to reject.

The final episode of *The Pyramid*, more complicated both structurally and psychologically, takes place over thirty years later during Oliver's first return to Stilbourne in a long time. His mother and his former music teacher, Miss Dawlish, called 'Bounce', are now dead. Oliver's mother, in the first two episodes, had repeatedly talked of how 'devoted' Oliver was to Miss Dawlish; it was also Miss Dawlish's car that Oliver had borrowed from the garageman, Henry, on the night he rescued Evie in the first episode. Now that 'Bounce' is dead, Oliver attempts to reconstruct her life both through and apart from local legend. A heavy and physically unattractive woman, she had been brought up by her demanding and tyrannical father, pushed into spending her life through music as compensation for any sort of sexual relationship, which her father assumed she could never enjoy. Her father drummed the lesson that 'Heaven is music'. When Henry Williams, an affable, feckless man who is capable in handling motor cars, arrives in Stilbourne, 'Bounce' is sufficiently charmed to buy a car she hardly needs and keep it in Henry's garage. After her father dies, she persuades Henry to move in with her, Henry bringing along his 'quite unforseen wife and child'. Henry cheerfully exploits 'Bounce', as she supports both his family and his rather seedy business for years; her music lessons are constantly disrupted by the storms of family life. Yet she continues to love Henry, to demand his attention even by devices like the frequent, semi-deliberate, minor car accidents caused by her incompetent driving. The town looks on the ménage with a condescending curiosity, especially amused and shocked by the difference in class between Henry and what they regard as the harmlessly eccentric Miss Dawlish. In retrospect, however, piecing together bits of her emotional explosions during music lessons which he remembers and the facts he now knows partly through the still surviving Henry, Oliver comes to understand something of the terror of repressed sexuality in which Miss Dawlish lived. He recognizes that he had never liked her, that his mother's assurances of his devotion were polite fabrications. But his current understanding now gives new meaning to the phrase that he was 'devoted' to her, a meaning as ironic and complex as is the phrase carved on her tombstone that 'Heaven is music'. Oliver sees, too, finally, although only in general terms that Golding does not specify, how the simplified inscriptions of Stilbourne have limited his own life.

The novel contains three episodes, all dramatising the narrowness and emptiness of Stilbourne life. Similarly, Stilbourne's sterility is visible in three different provinces of human experience: love, music and social class. Love represents human emotion, music human expression or achievement in art, and class human connections or relationships. All three are suppressed by Stilbourne, the condition of Golding's boyhood England. In a 1980 interview, Golding regarded the inhibition of class as the most crippling and significant:

It was about as stratified a society as you could well find anywhere in the country, and I think that the pyramidal structure of English society is present, and my awareness of it is indelibly imprinted in me, in my psyche, not merely in my intellect but very much in my emotional, almost my physical being. I am enraged by it and I am unable to escape it entirely, . . . It dissolves but it doesn't disappear; it's fossilised in me.[39]

Yet at the time he published *The Pyramid*, the centrality of the focus on class did not seem so indissolubly clear. He gave the novel an Egyptian epigraph: 'If thou be among people make for thyself love, the beginning and the end of the heart.' And the structure of all three of the episodes, like that of the novel itself, is a constant series of pyramids with 'love', in one form or another, at the base of each. The structure of the pyramid is also reflected in symbols apart from the stratifications of social class, like that of Miss Dawlish's metronome, finally ruined because the measures of music and art cannot compensate for love thwarted or deprived. The consciously Egyptian model that Golding used to structure his thought in the fiction perhaps seemed to him then to provide a more significant coherence, both structurally and psychologically, than does the sense of crippling class structure and its consequent social inhibition and waste that, for him now and for many of us reading the novel, seems to radiate from Stilbourne as his unique addition to a long chain of fictional treatments of the condition of England.

Golding's Egyptology and his location of his ideas in cultures and history apart from England's exercised an intermittent hold on his fictional imagination both in the construction of the metaphors of the earlier novels and in the geographical settings of some of his minor work. His first such locus for his fiction was not Egyptian but Classical, a 1956 novella called 'Envoy Extraordinary', published in a 1957 volume labelled on the cover a 'science fiction classic', entitled *Sometime, Never: Three Tales of Imagination*. The other two contributions were by John Wyndham and Mervyn Peake. 'Envoy Extraordinary' depicts a conflict between the sage humanistic wisdom of the Caesars, embodied in the old Emperor, and the scientific and rationalist perspective of an Alexandrian Greek inventor, Phanocles. This familiar Golding theme is made comic, sometimes even farcical as the inventions are disrupted by human misunderstanding and incompetence, and attached to a plot involving the succession of imperial power. Phanocles appeals to the Emperor to sponsor his inventions, particularly a ship propelled by steam. The Emperor is dubious, more interested in the pressure cooker Phanocles has also invented than in the steamship. But the Emperor's grandson, the young and ignorant Mamillius, who thinks that there cannot be a China because he does not know it, falls in love with Phanocles' beautiful and silent sister and helps persuade his grandfather to try the steamship. The 'Heir Designate' to the empire, Postumus, jealous and fearful that he may be displaced, sabotages the steamship. Other inventions, technologically sound, work no better in human terms. The invention of gunpowder is blocked by the brass butterfly of the firing pin, a symbol for human attraction to the random and the beautiful that contains an 'iron sting'. The invention of printing is blocked or diverted by the imaginative projection of what will be printed in the future, titles like 'The Unconscious Symbolism of the first book of Euclid' or 'Prologomena to the Investigation of Residual Trivia' through which Golding satirises academic investigation. In 'Envoy Extraordinary', the rational inventions are all finally comic and irrelevant, interesting attempts that the world cannot accept or use, diversions from the central concerns of the human being. By means other than the rational, the dangerous Postumus is defeated, the silly Mamillius is sent to China on a 'slow boat', and the wise old Emperor is to marry the inventor's beautiful sister.

'Envoy Extraordinary' is difficult to classify in terms that connect at all with the other fiction Golding was writing in the middle and late 1950s. Kingsley Amis, in his 1960 summary of science fiction entitled *New Maps of Hell*, suggested that Golding was the only serious current English novelist working within the genre of science fiction. Golding told an interviewer that he thought the general statement might apply to 'Envoy Extraordinary', but not to any of his other works,[40] which seems too literal and superficial a translation of the genre as metaphor than Amis may well have had in mind. Hoping to combine effectively the comedy, the drama of succession and the theme of conflict between rational invention and humane wisdom, Golding adapted the novella into a radio play for the BBC. Then, changing the title to *The Brass Butterfly*, he expanded it into a full-length play performed at the Strand Theatre in London in 1958 with Alastair Sim in the role of the Emperor. In changing novella to play, Golding made the dialogue more sharp and direct, more imitation Shaw in tone and argument, eliminating many of the metaphors in the characters' speech. He expanded the somewhat melodramatic role of the 'Heir Designate', reduced the silliness of Mamillius, and developed the minor character of Phanocles' sister into a major romantic figure (in the novella, her silence turned out to be the result of a hare-lip – a crudely farcical concept necessarily eliminated from the play). *The Brass Butterfly* was neither a great popular nor critical success. Golding also wrote several rather melodramatic radio plays: *Miss Pulkinhorn* (1960), the study of a woman (rather like Rowena Pringle in *Free Fall*) in a cathedral town who, torn between her own rigid orthodoxy and her mysticism that defies the established church, destroys both the play's version of the scapegoat saint and herself; and *Break My Heart*, a simplified version of the pattern of discovery of sin from *Free Fall* that takes place entirely within a boys' school.

This less 'essential', more committedly historical, aspect of Golding's imagination seemed to dangle without a coherent or appropriate form or focus except when it was subsumed into the metaphors of his major novels. The theme of the conflict between the rational or scientific world and that of the more mysterious or humane continued to fascinate Golding as he saw it expressed through historical ages. He continued to connect it with his early interest in Egyptology. In 1971, he republished 'Envoy Extraordinary' in a volume called *The Scorpion God*, along with two other novellas both set in ancient Egypt. Although 'Envoy Extraordinary''s setting is Roman rather than Egyptian, all three novellas share the comic tone, the issue of governance or control over a society, and the familiar tension between the rational and the mysterious. One of the new novellas is called 'The Scorpion God', and is concerned with the succession of the 'Great House' (a possible translation of the word 'Pharoah'). The ruler must run a race every seven years to justify his superiority over others, to prove that he is still the incarnation of the God who will make the river rise, a potency that is individual, economic and social. In the race that begins Golding's novella, the ruler is already going blind and his antagonist is a young man called 'The Liar' because he has other explanations for the river's rising, attributing it to snow melting in the mountains to the south. 'The Liar' is also already the lover of Princess 'Pretty Flower', a fact that in itself violates the Egyptian practice of confining royal love affairs to incest within the family, the consolidation of power. 'The Liar' wins in a race that is hardly fair, and he does not share the Eygptian ethos that advocates passive resignation to death. His principal conflict is with the priest, the 'Head Man', who insists on all the society's orthodoxies and builds his own rational texture of custom and control logically out of the implications of his observations. The 'Head Man' insists, for example, that the river's rise cannot be attributed to snow melting in the south because the south would have a sun even warmer than that of their snowless land. Yet 'The Liar' has more vision, more mystery, more life, and, in the final conflict, kills the 'Head Man' with the sting of the scorpion. The 'Head Man' is human, rational and ethical within the limits of his customary society; he is also the psychiatrist, in his final words explaining possible human motives for what 'The Liar' says and does. Yet, in terms of Golding's history, 'The Liar' is right in a higher, less psychologically and sociologically limited, sense; right about the insularity of the whole society and justified in his unethical means of securing power, just as he is right about the river's rising, although he cannot rationally explain how he knows what he does. 'The Liar' can see beyond the society's understanding of the human. In Golding's terms, he deserves the public and personal devotion of Princess 'Pretty Flower'. The other novella 'Clonk Clonk', like 'The Scorpion God', is full of characters' names as tags illustrating qualities, in this instance 'Fierce Eel', 'Furious Lion', 'Angry Elephant', 'Leopard Man', and 'Rutting Rhino' for the men and 'Palm' and various other trees, flowers and fish for the women. In 'Clonk Clonk', the individual and variously aggressive values of the men are in conflict with the concern for general content, survival and continuity expressed by the women in their adherence to community. The women, in a sense, are what they eat, what sustains them, while the men extend themselves rationally and egotistically beyond the boundaries of the women. The women win a war between the groups, and the values of community and acceptance, no matter how little understood rationally, are reasserted. Both of these novellas, gracefully comic and light in tone, are fables. They record a series of events that demonstrate simple moral truths, in both these instances the limitations of confident, individual rationality and the wisdom of acceptance of communal warmth and mystery. These convey the simple prescriptive truths that Golding's richer, more dense and impacted metaphors qualify and deepen. And that sense of fable, for Golding, is connected finally with the Egyptology of his imagination, with an historical sense far removed from the complexities of contemporary experience.

For a number of years after this minor work, Golding published no fiction. But, as early as 1974, he mentioned intending to write a major novel 'about England'.[41] From the perspective of his later fiction, Golding's Egyptology always had been a charming, learned and individualistic diversion from the major interest in making a comprehensive social statement about his own world, about the condition of England with a range and in a form less limited than that of *The Pyramid*. The result of this long period of gestation, *Darkness Visible* (1979), is Golding's most ambitious novel, with its title from Milton's Satan surveying his world just after the Fall and its epigraph from Virgil's Aeneas praying that he be allowed to report on the nature of the Underworld.[42] The allusions, however, unlike those in the Egyptian fable, are serious indicators of the direction and depth of the treatment of England over a span of nearly forty years of recent historical time. Golding's panoramic treatment is large, bizarre and visionary, both eventful and constantly metaphorical. Unlike the intense, confined metaphors of the earlier fiction, *Darkness Visible* sprawls, both in themes and techniques, to include the complexity and variety of contemporary experience. Just as in Elizabeth Bowen's rather similarly sprawling contemporary vision, *Eva Trout*, no single tidy, linear or coherent shape, no single plane of treatment or perspective, seems able to accommodate, either literally or metaphorically, all the experience central to Golding's 1979 contribution to the literary genre of the condition of England.

Darkness Visible begins with a scene of apocalypse. From a raging London firestorm during the bombing of the Second World War, a 'red curtain of flame' with 'a white heart of fire' that is 'melting lead and distorting iron', a small child mysteriously emerges, the left side of his face burning, as the firefighters and rescuers watch. The nameless child inexplicably survives the searing fire, the pathway of all the 'secondary explosions of gas and fuel', and 'the kind of first aid for burns

which is reversed by the medical profession every year or so'
(Chapter I). Called at first just no. 7, though finally given the
name of Matty by a compassionate hospital staff to which he
owes his life, he survives deformed and anonymous as part of
the issue of the Second World War itself. Golding had
apparently originally written a similar scene of firestorm,
equally intense and powerful, to function symbolically in the
same way as a preface to *Lord of the Flies*, but in discussion with
his publisher eliminated it before publication.[43] The scene in
Darkness Visible, however, is both a piece of frightening and
compelling metaphorical prose and sufficient cause for a world
that is depicted as terrifyingly different from the one it replaced.

When Matty leaves the hospital, the left side of his face is
permanently swollen and deformed, he has no left ear, and his
mouth is so misshapen he has difficulty speaking. He is sent to
a school for foundlings in the village of Greenfield where his
deformities and difficulties in speaking make him the butt of
most of the boys. Sebastian Pedigree, a repressed homosexual
master who is revolted by Matty's appearance, is warned by
the headmaster about rumours concerning his behaviour and
partiality, and so stops the extra lessons for his attractive
favourite boy to give Matty special tutorials as a penance. The
favourite, rejected, commits suicide. Pedigree is dismissed and
imprisoned, irrationally blaming Matty for his disgrace, and
Matty, inarticulate and confused in trying to explain to the
headmaster what he thinks had happened, is sent away from
the school as hopelessly stupid. Golding then begins to relate a
series of picaresque incidents in which Matty is always rejected,
always on the outside. He works in a vast old-fashioned
hardware shop, then migrates to Australia for various jobs in
both city and outback. As he grows older, still invariably the
scapegoat, he experiences sexual feelings and begins to read the
Bible obsessively to quench his sexual desire. He becomes a
religious mystic. In a grotesquely comic incident, which Matty
entirely misunderstands, an Australian aboriginal, full of anger,
jumps on Matty's groin when Matty draws an elaborate cross
with pebbles. The aboriginal thinks Matty has arranged the
pebbles as a marker to British planes to begin nuclear testing.
Matty, maimed again, thinks himself rendered permanently
impotent in what Golding calls a 'crucifarce'. Yet however
ludicrous and misunderstood the literal experience, its effect is

to underline Matty's role as victim. He then lines the pebbles of his huge cross with twigs and sets the twigs on fire, disrupting traffic in a public gesture that is taken as a protest against nuclear arms. He is deported, wanders across the United States, and then returns to England to settle in Cornwall, keeping a journal that will lead up to and explain the religious apocalypse to take place on 6/6/66, the number of the Anti-Christ or the Devil. When nothing noteworthy happens on 6 June 1966, Matty takes a job as an assistant gardener and handyman at a posh public school in Greenfield, near the school of foundlings. Although he is still a mystic, an outsider who hears voices, and desires to save some of the young people he sees, Matty's behaviour is now less eccentric than it was and he works happily and efficiently at the school for ten years. In the meantime, Pedigree, released from prison and unable to find another job as a master, returns to Greenfield to try to expiate his guilt. Like Matty, he is a scapegoat, fragmented in form (as the narratives describing both Matty and Pedigree are frequently fragmented) and constantly misunderstood by the community.

Mutual misunderstanding is axiomatic in Golding's version of the contemporary world. At one point, he stands aside to comment that:

> People find it remarkable when they discover how little one man knows about another. Equally, at the very moment when people are most certain that their actions and thoughts are most hidden in darkness, they often find out to their astonishment and grief how they have been performing in the bright light of day and before an audience. (Chapter II)

The second part of the proposition, the most visible aspect of the darkness, is detailed in the long narrative of Part Two of the novel, the story of Sophy. This story is structurally and in some ways thematically parallel to the story of Matty. Like Matty, Sophy is an issue of the Second World War, but she is the product of its social dislocations rather than its physical terrors. She is one of a set of extremely attractive twins who grow up in Greenfield with their father and his mistress, a former 'au pair' girl, after their mother has abandoned them and left her failed marriage for New Zealand. Sophy and her sister Toni are like 'night and day', Sophy, the dark one,

mysteriously attractive and apparently impenetrable, Toni, the
very fair one, transparent, who is far more indifferent to all the
instability and shifting alliances among the older generation.
Just as their father is about to marry the 'au pair' girl, the
twins discover her infidelity with an 'uncle', another surrogate
relationship in the twins' world in which 'aunties' and 'uncles'
abound. Sophy, jealous and physically attracted to her frequently
remote or absent father, tells him of the 'au pair''s infidelity.
Toni leaves, going with friends to Afghanistan where she is
caught with a gang running drugs, then, after a short sojourn at
home, travelling to find meaning and excitement in Cuba and
the Near East. She simply escapes, whereas Sophy, darker, with
more subterranean motives and more attached to and angry at
her father, stays close to home, wanting both to express the
darkness she feels inside herself and to get back at the
respectable daylight world that she feels has deprived and
injured her. She separates herself from conventional meaning,
as she hitch-hikes on the motorway to lose her virginity in the
most casual way possible. When she is bored working for a
travel agency in London, she begins an affair with a dull,
respectable man who wants to marry her. But she is able to
achieve orgasm only when she stabs him with a tiny knife, and
she then begins a more violent kind of sex life with a man she
has met in a disco. Her life with her new man leads to
considerable traffic in drugs and crime. Golding is depicting a
nightmarish world of the contemporary young, victims and
victimizers alike. Sophy is never the scapegoat; rather, through
all these incidents, she is passionately self-absorbed, the
demanding ego who imposes her will on others and cares only
for self-satisfaction. She both bitterly resents and physically
desires her father, unable to separate or understand her own
frequently explosive emotions. Sophy suggests to her crowd
that they kidnap and hold for ransom an Arab princeling who
attends the school where Matty works – one of Sophy's crowd
is the Physical Education instructor at the school. Although
some are sceptical or frightened of such a direct assault on
civilisation, Sophy, as always imposing her will, insists and uses
her sexuality to gain assent for her deeper and more entirely
personal gratification.

Part Three brings all the characters and themes together in a
further rush of incident, complex motive and violent action.

Greenfield in 1978 is described as full of muddled, trivial, dislocated people, harrassed by the incessant noise of traffic and jet planes and divided into antagonistic racial groups. Greenfield is called an echo of the past and a centre with no sense of community or feeling for others. Against the background, Matty and Pedigree finally meet in the local bookstore and hesitantly develop the beginnings of some understanding of each others' past and motives. The twins' father, still isolated emotionally, thinks his daughters and their generation totally corrupt, dangerous, 'beastly little monsters' who have tried to poison him (Chapter XIII). Sophy leaves her engagement ring under a tree at the school, part of her plot to have an excuse to return. Matty finds the ring, tries to reclaim it, to 'save' the situation, as he vaguely recognises something of the deliberate plot. The night of the kidnapping is a fiasco of mistakes, violence, random assaults and a cataclysmic fire, another apocalypse. Watching the fire from a distance, Sophy recognises fully her own darkness: 'Suddenly she knew it was her own fire, a thing she had done, a proclamation, a deed in the eye of the world – an outrage, a triumph! The feeling stormed through her, laugher, fierceness, a wild joy at the violation' (Chapter XV). In the midst of this exultation, she expresses her darkness at its deepest extremity and kills, with a commando knife, the Arab boy who has been bound in the lavatory where he, like Beatrice Ifor in *Free Fall*, urinated on the floor in fright. The whole school and parts of the town burn in the fire.

Yet, even though Golding does a scene of the subsequent trial of Sophy and her crowd for terrorism and murder, we never learn the whole story. Sophy's father, for example, may or may not really have loved or cared for his daughters. As numerous characters on the fringes of the town or school report, one can never bring it all together, never apportion cause or blame precisely, never fully understand all that has happened in the modern world: 'One is one and all alone and ever more shall be so' (Chapter XIII); 'No one will *ever* know what happened. There's too much of it, too many people, a sprawling series of events that break apart under their own weight' (Chapter XV).

Yet some particular fates and gestures can be understood. During the action, Matty is knocked unconscious by one of the terrorists as a diversionary tactic. But a bomb accidentally

explodes in a petrol tank starting the fire, and, although the boy
Matty had emerged from fire nearly forty years earlier, this time
the man cannot. The scapegoat is engulfed in flames. The only
product of his sacrifice, the only redemption, is, ironically, that of
Pedigree whose actions had set Matty off on his wanderings. After
the trial and its inconclusiveness, while sitting in the village park,
Pedigree, generally regarded as parasitic and harmlessly eccentric
now, begins to cry and commune with the dead Matty. He
realises, in surprise, 'that it should be you, ugly little Matty, who
really loved me! I tried to throw it away you know, but it wouldn't
go. Who are you Matty?' Matty is, of course, the potentially
redemptive Christ figure, the selfless victim sacrificing himself for
all human ego, and therefore radiating love for another. Pedigree
recognises that the image of Matty has given him 'freedom' as well
as love, and, in Pedigree's vision, Matty's face is finally
transformed:

> For the golden immediacy of the wind altered at its heart and
> began first to drift upwards, then swirl upwards then rush
> upwards round Matty. The gold grew fierce and burned.
> Sebastian watched in terror as the man before him was
> consumed, melted, vanished like a guy in a bonfire; and the
> face was no longer two-tone but gold as the fire and stern
> and everywhere there was a sense of the peacock eyes of great
> feathers and the smile round the lips was loving and terrible.
> (Chapter XVI)

The passage carries metaphorical echoes of both the Bible and
T. S. Eliot's *Four Quartets*. Sebastian Pedigree is found dead on
the park bench by the keeper.

Golding's religious vision and his vision of moral depravity
and selfishness combine to create a blistering indictment of
contemporary England. The 'darkness' cogently and
meticulously made visible in this, Golding's most extensive and
ambitious treatment of the current condition of England, is a
searing and horrifying depiction of ego; the light is only
transposed imagination, manifest only in outsiders, the feeble,
the maimed and the ugly. The older England of Stilbourne was
sterile, all human feeling repressed by convention, trivia, and
social stratification. But the newer, more liberated England of

the no longer accurately named Greenfield is grotesque, a collection of violent and random assaults committed by vast numbers of isolated selves. A healthy sense of community and caring for others is violated even more forcefully by the random imposing egos than it was by the lethal stratifications and hypocrisies of class. Golding frames his development of the condition of England over the past forty years with the two apocalyptic fires, two transformations that destroy an old world and create a new one. The first fire, the Second World War, consumed Stilbourne and brought forth, almost miraculously, a maimed, deformed but vital new birth. Yet the emerging world, in its ego and nearly total dedication to self-satisfaction, rejected the agent of salvation that the initial community, the hospital and fire-fighters of 1940, had worked so hard to save. Matty cannot survive the second fire in any form other than the questionable transcendental, visible as metaphor only to those similarly maimed, guilty and rejected. The evasive and hypocritical social stratifications of Stilbourne have become, in Golding's perspective of 1979, the still more rigid Greenfield stratifications of multiple egos that reject everything outside the self.

Golding's version of the condition of England may not command wide assent. Extrapolated into social commentary or regarded as social analysis, his Englands, both Stilbourne and Greenfield, can seem extreme and overstated, one the product of the excessively moralistic young rebel, the other that of the moralistic old curmudgeon. Golding is still, in this novel, more interested in ideas than he is in people. His undescribed value of community can also linger as a nostalgic or sentimental gesture for a shared value that never was visible in any actual condition of England, or was visible only as a momentary and circumstantial phenomenon in 1940. Yet literal accuracy, if such is ever possible, or analysis, is hardly the point. Rather, Golding's literary strength is the complex and emotionally evocative appeal of his powerful prose, as effective in parts of *Darkness Visible* as it is in *Lord of the Flies*, *Pincher Martin*, or *The Spire*. The passages describing the fires, Sophy's apprehension of her darkness, and the visions of saintly transcendence create, with brilliance and complexity, an essence of human emotional experience. A similar passage in *Darkness Visible* is one in which Matty, in Australia, is wondering about the appropriate natural

setting and basis in landscape for the construction of his large
cross of stones:

> Then, accustomed to the darkness by a long enough stay and
> willing – it would have to be by sacrifice of life and limb – to
> trade everything for the sight, the eyes would find what
> evidence there was for them too. It might be a faint
> phosphorescence round the fungi on the trunks of trees that
> had fallen and were not so much rotting as melting away, or
> the occasional more lambent blueness where the flames of
> marsh gas wandered among reeds and floating islands of
> plants that lived as much on insects as on soupy water.
> Sometimes and suddenly as if they were switched on, the
> lights would be more spectacular still – a swift flight of
> sparks flashing between tree trunks, dancing, turning into a
> cloud of fire that twisted in on itself, broke, became a
> streamer leading away which incomprehensibly switched
> itself off to leave the place even darker than before. Then
> perhaps with a sigh like a sleeper turning over, a big thing
> would move washily in the unseen water and loiter a little
> further away. By then, feet that had stayed that long would
> have sunk deep, the mud moving to this side and that, the
> warm mud; and the leeches would have attached themselves
> down there in an even darker darkness, a more secret secrecy
> and with unconscious ingenuity, and without allowing their
> presence to be felt would have begun to feed through the
> vulnerable skin. (Chapter V)

Golding's passages of this kind of complex descriptive prose,
combining the strikingly physical with emanations of the
spiritual, suggest something of the contradictory emotional
qualities of T. S. Eliot's later poetry and the descriptions in
some of Thomas Hardy's novels without imitating either.
Golding's social and religious visions, like his metaphors for the
essence of man, are finally justified through their emotionally
powerful prose. The prose itself conveys the range and intensity
of the myths of man or of society that the novels try to convey.
The writing is the appeal and the justification of *Darkness
Visible*, as it is of the earlier metaphors as novel, and becomes,
in both of Golding's subsequent and most recent works,
metaphorically the subject of the fiction itself.

6

The Condition of the Writer:
Rites of Passage and
The Paper Men

Despite its devastating implications as commentary about the current condition of England, *Darkness Visible*, like all Golding's fiction, is visionary rather than analytical and describes an interior state of mind and emotion. As Golding had said in 1970, when explaining why he thought writers of fiction did not write about what they knew or were sure of: 'Writing is not reportage, but imagination.'[44] Golding's fiction has always been that of the self-enclosed 'imagination'. With increasing experience as a writer, however, in the fiction that follows *Darkness Visible*, *Rites of Passage* only one year later in 1980 and then *The Paper Men* in 1984, the 'imagination' becomes implicitly and then explicitly that of the writer. The 'imagination' is literary and consciously self-creative rather than the imagination of the thoughtful iconoclast or the seer.

In recognising his own literary focus, however, Golding still maintains a strong sense of individuality that both uses and resists the conventional implications of various literary forms. For example, in an address given in France in 1977, he defined himself in opposition to the writer of the utopia, the form that conventionally gives literary meaning or vision to extensive social commentary, which the writer uses to construct a social world. Golding claimed that he had finally defined himself as an 'antiutopian', and that he 'felt like the gentleman who had been speaking prose all his life'. Similarly, he rejected the reverse definition, diagnosis 'as a "dystopist"' because 'setting aside the questionable etymology of the word, it seemed to describe some terrible disease or perhaps a vice so disgusting its name was not to be found in the dictionary'.[45] The deflection into the only tangentially relevant is characteristic Golding, although it indicates his resistance to the social and philosophical implications of conventional forms, his insistence that what is important about human beings goes beyond any social system or construction that can be articulated by or reflected in literary form. The definitions of 'antiutopian' and 'dystopist' also illustrate a process relevant to Golding's use of literary form in *Rites of Passage* and *The Paper Men*. Literary form, in these novels concerned with the condition and the imagination of the writer, functions as the target, the propellant to be reversed in the fictional explosion that follows, in a more extended and complex way than the targets or propellants of Ballantyne and Wells functioned for *Lord of the Flies* and *The Inheritors*.

Rites of Passage begins with the form of reportage, the recording journal like that of the earliest eighteenth-century English novels. The recorder, Edmund Talbot, is a rather scrupulous and pedantic young man on a ship during a lull in the Napoleonic Wars headed toward Australia where he is to take up a position in colonial administration. He is educated and snobbish, full of Greek quotations and judgements about the manners of his travelling companions. References to the superior civilisation at Oxford crowd his reflections, as do statements about his confidence in the colonising mission of the English: 'Long live illusion, say I. Let us export it to our colonies with all the other benefits of civilisation!' (Section 51). At the same time, he is curious about everything happening on the ship, anxious to talk to everyone he can, and he sees the ship in terms that apply to it both as an engineering marvel and as an assemblage of diverse people, a 'harmony' that 'has more strings than a violin, more than a lute, more I think than a harp, and under the wind's tuition she makes a ferocious music' (Section 2). He sees the other passengers and crew as types, as if they are characters representative of social entities in an eighteenth-century picaresque: the sternly atheistic captain in total command of ship, the grotesquely self-indulgent artist, the provocative and painted whore, the feeble and classless parson who embarrasses the others with his emotions, the handsome, adaptable, and totally amoral seaman. Even when something the other characters say or do questions the allegiance to type, Talbot's commentary safely restores them to their social role.

Talbot's journal is also full of literary reference. He begins by announcing his interest in 'lively old Fielding and Smollett', these having replaced his earlier interest, apparently generated by his father, in 'sentimental Goldsmith and Richardson' (Section 1). He can now 'no longer credit Mistress *Pamela*'s pietistic accounts of every shift in her calculated resistance to the advances of her master!' (Section 4). When he and the whore, Zenobia, engage in mutual seduction in his cabin: 'The bookshelf tilted. *Moll Flanders* lay open on the deck, *Gil Blas* fell on her and my aunt's parting gift to me, Hervey's *Meditations among the Tombs (MDCCLX) II vols London* covered them both' (Section 30). The most pervasive and significant literary reference, however, is to the emergence of a new sensibility, to Coleridge's *Rime of the Ancient Mariner*. At first, Zenobia quotes the passage of 'All, all alone', with a deliberate and mocking theatricality. Talbot agrees with her lack of sentimentality, equating Coleridge with superstition. As the ship nears the Equator, Talbot confidently thinks the legend silly:

> In fact I found that Mr. Coleridge had been mistaken. Sailors are superstitious indeed, but careless of life in any direction. The only reason why they do not shoot seabirds is first because they are not allowed weapons and second because seabirds are not pleasant to eat. (Section 30)

But as the novel develops, and as Talbot's rationalistic journal is replaced by a long letter from Colley, the feeble parson, read after his death, the function of Coleridge's legend changes. Colley, the scapegoat, has understood, in terms different from those in the literary model, the meaning of sailors' superstitions and the psychological implications of 'all alone'. Even Talbot, in his final response to the multiple revelations in Colley's letter, one of Golding's characteristic codas to his novels, tells the most sympathetic of the ship's officers: 'Life is a formless business, . . . Literature is much amiss in forcing a form on it!' Like literature generally, Talbot's self-consciously rational and observant journal has recorded very little of the intellectual or emotional truth of the life through which he has sailed.

Another literary form, that of drama, is central to both
Talbot's journal and Colley's letter. The crucial dramatic
incident is the mystery of what happened to Colley in the
fo'castle among the common sailors, at the ceremony for
crossing the Equator, that led him subsequently to die of
'shame'. References to drama are frequent in the conversation
and events leading up to the crucial incident, although, as
Talbot remarks several times in his journal, he cannot
distinguish tragedy from farce in regard to what he sees
happening on the ship. He is inclined to regard all theatre as
farce, and invariably remarks on the theatrical postures of
passengers and crew: the parades and posing of Zenobia and
the other passengers, the captain's hatred of all religion and
religious symbols, Colley dressing 'in a positive delirium of
ecclesiastical finery . . . quite simply silly under our vertical
sun' as he goes ostensibly to preach a sermon to the seamen.
Talbot makes constant comparisons to the Greeks, confident
that what happens must be seen as farce because it all lacks the
dignity of tragedy. He is inclined to think Colley's 'shame' a
feeble and ridiculously sensitive response to the Captain's
hatred of religion and his possible nastiness or acrimony when
Colley is determined to preach to the seamen – in Talbot's
frame of reference, a disastrous farce created by the opposition
of two irrational dogmas. But Talbot, in the insularity of his
class and his canons of taste, misses the fact that the drama is
one of class. The social lines on board ship are rigidly stratified,
and Golding has, in an essay called 'A Touch of Insomnia'
written several years before the novel appeared, satirically
commented at length on the visible and rigid demarcations of
class on transatlantic liners: 'Where you were born, there you
stayed.'[46] In *Rites of Passage*, the fo'castle is lower-class territory,
ruled by the handsome and spontaneous seaman Billy Rogers.
Talbot, like Oliver in *The Pyramid* initially, cannot imagine that
life among the lower orders could be any different from life in the
sheltered cabins of the upper classes. He does not see the point
when the seamen, in an earlier ceremony, parody the gestures and
the play of the upper classes; he thinks the seamen are simply
emulating their betters as role models but doing it crudely, when
in fact they are performing and undercutting with deliberate
derision. Drama, the most public literary form, makes
relationships visible, publicises the stratifications and the fractures

of English class society. When the ship crosses the Equator, the crucial ceremony to mark the voyage into an unknown or reversed world, Talbot assumes that the overdressed Colley has gone to the fo'castle to preach to save the seamen, or beg them to repent, to disseminate universal salvation as a gift from upper orders to lower in what is, after all, a supremely silly context. For Talbot, this is comedy, farce, a foolish and dogmatic man grossly miscalculating his connections with and disconnections from others. Colley's letter, however, later reveals what Talbot even then can barely understand, that Colley was called into the fo'castle by the seamen for their own ceremony, a ritual in which he was the scapegoat, the enemy, the vulnerable spot in the carapace of the upper classes, the psychological identity beneath the divisions of class, and the 'victim of their cruel sport'.

The narrative of Colley's letter is another literary form, counter to Talbot's journal. Talbot discovers the letter which Colley had written to his sister back in England, but he is convinced he cannot forward it and must, like Conrad's Marlow for Kurtz's 'intended' at the end of *Heart of Darkness*, compose convenient and civilised lies (the use of Conrad as posing a class and moral problem for the civilised European recurs throughout Golding's fiction). Colley's letter is emotional and self-pitying, in the first instance an expression of the human body. He is often ill, physically unattractive, and his 'uncommonly public micturation' resembles drunkenness and is shocking to most of the other passengers. He also notices and finds 'intolerable' all the effluvias that surround the ship when it is becalmed. His letter betrays his naïveté about the other passengers (for example, he thinks Zenobia a 'young lady of great piety and beauty'), and recounts his argument with the Captain over whether or not he has permission to preach to the seamen. Colley sees the Captain as cold and indifferent, rejecting him and religion, but not shaming him or frightening him, certainly not cause for strong emotional reaction. Through the letter, the deficiencies and shallowness of Talbot's journal become visible, for Colley, describing many of the same incidents without reference to manners or class, has a more cogent sense of the meaning of human behaviour and far more sympathy for others, even his antagonists. Talbot's journal is the record of an educated misplaced confidence, as if superficial man could sustain conscious control over and trivial judgement about his environment; Colley's letter, more emotional and on its

surface more unattractive, is the subterranean document, man
more deeply responsive to others and out of conscious control. In a
way, too, the forms are historical generalisations, Talbot's the
reasoned, calm document of the Neo-Classical age, Colley's the
dark mystery, expressed in both cosmic and psychological terms,
of the age of the Romantics. In dealing with the spiritual or the
religious world, Talbot's is the voice of sane and complacent
scepticism, Colley's that of passionate although sometimes vague
and confused commitment.

Colley's letter also gradually reveals his growing attraction to
Talbot. Although Talbot is condescending and rather coolly
polite in all their interchanges, Colley begins to regard him as
representing a finer and nobler humanity. When Talbot is
seasick and sleeping off his malady, Colley sneaks into his
cabin, views him as Christ-like, and, 'in some irresistible
compulsion', bends down and kisses his hand because he does
not feel himself worthy of the 'holiness' of Talbot's lips. Only
vaguely aware that his attractions or compulsions are
homosexual, Colley is also attracted to others, particularly to
the seaman, Billy Rogers. Colley's compulsion to preach is his
desire to connect with others and, when again politely ignored
by Talbot in his upper-class remoteness, he turns his attention
to the men in the fo'castle. They are more direct, less removed,
and they summon Colley to their ceremony, their public and
merciless parody of what they see as the drama and interchange
of upper-class emotion. Colley must approach the 'throne', on
which the handsome Billy Rogers is seated, and must then kneel
in worship and abase himself in committing the act of *fellatio*.
The seamen find the ceremony uproariously funny, a scapegoat
from the supposed upper classes reduced to behaving like the
unmannered and amoral animals the men know they are;
Colley, never having known or faced the implications of his
latent homosexuality before and finding himself involved in a
direct experience he cannot convert to some form of spiritual
meaning, dies of 'shame'. Later, at the ship's official inquest
into Colley's death, the Captain, seeking to defend the class
system and apportion blame, accuses Rogers of 'buggery'.
Rogers accepts the charge, then licks his lips mockingly and
asks if he should begin with the officers. Charges are dismissed,
and nothing else is said – no further acknowledgement of

human depravity need be articulated in verbal form. Only Colley's letter has come close to giving form to the unacknowledgeable depths of human experience, and that is at the price of clarity, of focus, of an exterior composure and control, and finally, of the form of human life itself.

The death of Colley and the partial dissemination of its implications among passenger and crew have some influence on the community of the ship. Miss Granham, for example, the hitherto repressed, militantly commonsensical and mannered governness and the sceptical and grudging Mr Prettiman are able to decide to marry. Talbot also learns a little more than he knew before. He is able to recognise that in some symbolic way Colley's emotional vulnerability did represent a possibly meaningful 'salvation' of the sunderings of class that neither Talbot nor the other passengers could follow. He can see Colley as the vague antithesis to the purser, a figure mysteriously remote in the bowels of the ship throughout the voyage. At the end, Talbot sees and depicts the purser, the keeper of the tools and money on which the ship's form of civilisation depends, as a kind of devil figure presiding over an underworld. Talbot also recognises the irony and hypocrisy in the lies he finally writes to Colley's sister, the irony in realising that he is representing a supposedly just administration of civilisation: 'How is that for a start to a career in the service of my King and Country?' Colley's 'service' has been more genuine, more concerned with others, but it cost him first his dignity and then his life. No salvation is achieved in the novel, no resolution of the issues, physical or spiritual, that Colley's story dramatised. In addition, although the pieces of writing come closer to giving coherence to experience, no work of writing itself is able to express or convey all the complexities of experience – not Talbot's mannered and distant rational journal, not Colley's subterranean and ruminative letter. The writings are forms through which the writer must work, forms that themselves become the always partial and equivocal subject of the fiction. Yet Golding's perspective, neither that of Talbot nor Colley, unable to resolve the issues that emerge through those narratives, is that of the writer working both through and against the forms of writing he establishes. Golding arrives as closely as he can to what he sees as social, communal and religious experience through the consideration of literature and writing, through a use and examination of the forms which simplify, which only feebly and partially represent, the condition of the human being.

The negativity of Golding's approach, the impulsive perversity in most often outlining a subject, at least initially, through what it is not, continues to characterise his career. As Golding indicates in his preface to *A Moving Target*, he is inclined to be self-protective about explaining the complexities in his fiction. He dislikes teaching, dislikes the pose of the lecturer in which he finds himself 'wooing the audience, being at once shamelessly timid and modestly boastful', and he particularly dislikes abandoning the form of fiction through which his mind and emotions most deeply and characteristically work. For both others and himself, he wants to guard the conventions of fiction, 'the unrealities to which the audience assent in advance so that they may be ushered into the presence of more vivid reality'. He notes that others call this 'the willing suspension of disbelief', but he thinks 'it might be more accurate to call it the substitution of one level of belief for another'.[47] The 'level of belief' continues to operate in fictional terms in Golding's next novel, *The Paper Men*. But, whereas the subject of *Rites of Passage* was the fiction itself, the nature of narrative, journal or letter, the subject of *The Paper Men* is the practitioner of fiction, the writer. In a way, this is a more risky, more difficult subject, for audiences seeing characterisations of people used as centrally representative in a fiction concocted by a person can easily confuse 'one level of belief for another'. To begin *The Paper Men*, Golding established the persona of Wilfred Barclay, an aging, successful, sometimes mystical, self-absorbed and curmudgeonly novelist, to propel his consideration of the writer. Many of the initial readers and reviewers confused the persona with the author, converted fictional belief into personal belief, and regarded the exploration of Wilfred Barclay as Golding's thorny, belligerent defence of himself and his privacy. Those readers took a speculation about literary biography, about the nature of the writer, as querulous and undigested autobiography, and, in consequence, tended to dismiss the novel.

Wilfred Barclay, at the beginning of the novel, is bored with and angry at the American Assistant Professor of English Literature from the University of Astrakhan, Rick L. Tucker, who has achieved his reputation by counting the number of relative clauses Barclay has used in his novels as an index to his style. Tucker now wants to write Barclay's biography. In relentless pursuit of any scrap of paper relevant to Barclay's life, Tucker keeps exerting pressure on Barclay to sign a paper authorising his status as the official biographer, a documentation Barclay resists. The incidents are handled in a tone of comic outrage, an expansion of the outrageous farce of some of Golding's earlier works. When, one night, Barclay hears scuffling among his dustbins, he runs out, his pyjamas slipping to his knees, and shoots what he disingenuously assumes is a raiding badger to find that he has slightly wounded Tucker, the badger rummaging for bits of paper that Barclay may have discarded. The incident leads Liz, Barclay's wife, to discover a different scrap of paper, part of a letter to Barclay from another woman that leads her to divorce him. As Barclay wanders Europe and the Mediterranean, trying to hide in places like an isolated mountain top in the Swiss Alps, still badgered for his signature by Tucker, he recalls much of his seedy past. He has been entirely egotistical, a debased and more grotesquely comic Pincher Martin or Sammy Mountjoy, through a career as a bad bank clerk, a dishonest journalist, a self-serving naval man during the war, numerous adulterous affairs with women, and sudden accidental success as a novelist. Tucker brings his wife Mary Lou, a beautiful and spectrally silent figure, to the stage setting in the Alps, Mary Lou trying to seduce Barclay into signing, an incident that leaves Barclay full of contradictory guilts. He feels guilty at the waste in having rejected Mary Lou, for she radiates an unusually spiritual beauty; he also feels guilty because he is so corruptible. The outrageousness is also extended to the outside world, like Barclay's author's club in London in which the Victorian statue to Psyche, the image of soul, has been replaced by contemporary statues directly representing and glorifying incest and homosexuality. All the outrage, excess and contradiction in Barclay's voice indicate that he is an extremely unreliable narrator, one who sees himself alternately as martyr, devil, saint, victim and beleaguered paranoid hero. Clearly, the voice is not Golding's or in any way a personal autobiographical statement when Barclay speculates about whether or not to sign in the following characteristic terms:

At one point I had Tucker writing my biography but with
such strict supervision it included for the world's inspection
an account of how he had attempted the virtue of St Wilfred
with the offer of his beautiful wife; an offer rejected with such
gentle tact and kindness that he (Assistant Professor Rick L.
Tucker) flung himself on his knees and received such a
gigantic hack in his privates from one of those boots that were
no good for rough country he immediately entered a monastery,
leaving his beautiful wife to – Yes, I was unbalanced, there's no
doubt about it. But the dope was good and I wish I knew what it
was. (Chapter IX)

Barclay is a seedier Sammy Mountjoy without ambition or
purpose; Tucker is, perhaps, a comically reversed, meaningless,
and even more grotesque Parson Colley.

In so far as the novel has a metaphorical structure, the
drama mimics that of Faust. Barclay initially seems to have the
role of the tempted Faust, even though he quotes the phrase,
'Why, this is Hell, nor am I out of it', that Christopher
Marlowe gives to Mephistophelis. Tucker's role is more that of
Mephistophelis, the tempter, the agent of the Devil. The Devil,
perhaps, is Halliday, an American banker, billionaire and
collector who never appears in the novel but finances Tucker's
pursuit. Halliday, in the words of the critic Don Crompton, is
'a spiritual accountant as sinister and elusive as the purser in
Rites of Passage'.[48] But the application of Faustian metaphor or
drama quickly breaks down, for it is impossible, in any
meaningful way, to distinguish tempter from victim, Devil from
man, corrupted for corruptible. In the first instance, Barclay
hoards his own paper, scraps, letters, all the trivia of his life
and his career as an author. The novel extends, and when, in
time, Tucker stops pursuing Barclay, Barclay is at first
distraught, then reverses the roles and phones Tucker to meet
him at the same hotel in the Swiss Alps where Barclay had
earlier rejected Tucker's insistence that he sign. Time has
clearly passed, for Mary Lou is now living with Halliday and
the social world has moved into the late 1960s, Tucker wearing
his hair in a dyed Afro, white trousers 'flared at the bottom and
the gores were sequinned', and a vest with 'a huge chunk
carved out of it clear down to where his navel would have been
in view if that thatch, coppice, undergrowth of Tuckerish hair

hadn't hidden it.' (Chapter XII). Golding also reveals that an earlier episode, during their first encounter in the Alps, was not as Barclay had thought it. Climbing in the fog one day, over what Tucker had said was a precipitous ledge, Barclay slipped and thought he had been rescued by Tucker, a claim on his gratitude and being that, in his defiant guilt and defensiveness, he was determined to resist. During the later meeting in the Alps, in bright sunshine, Barclay sees that the ledge is suspended only a few feet above a soft, pleasant meadow, and he consequently turns the guilt that generated the situation against himself and his symbolic desire to be rescued. The hoax, like the pursuit, works both ways, and, during the later meeting in the Alps, Barclay finally signs the paper granting Tucker the permission to write the official biography.

The two become locked in a power struggle of negotiations, trading and arguing about documents, rights, or their support by Mary Lou and by Halliday. Who owns or has the right to what is suspended in comedy or outrage. As Barclay says: 'In fact, the biography will be a duet, Rick. We'll show the world what we are – paper men, you can call us. How about that for a title?' (Chapter XII). The symbiosis is that of the writer, two only apparently different practitioners of fiction, novelist and biographer, pursued and pursuer, both finally existing only in terms of their detritus, their paper. On an ancillary level, Golding also suggests that the symbiosis is referentially cultural and national. What seemed to begin as satire of American academic pretence and vapidity (Mary Lou, for example, has a degree in flower-arranging and bibliography) from a sane, traditional, commonsensical English point of view turns into a constantly linked transfer, each exchanging with the other the trivia of clothes, customs and commodities of his particular culture. Cultural integrity, in Golding's terms, is as rare and unlikely as personal integrity or integrity among writers, each trapping itself or himself in the opposite which is its twin. Issues of good or evil, sin or temptation, Faustian issues, are never resolved in a drama in which, finally, one outcropping of the communal culture, or one paper man, cannot be distinguished from another.

Toward the end of the novel, the outrageousness, the sense of man at his comic and cosmic extremes, escalates markedly. Barclay and Tucker get into a farcical and violent fight over

who owns which trivial document in Barclay's London club.
Just before this, Barclay returns to Liz, now that her other man
has left. But Liz is older, full of rage, which is also cancer, and
when, as a last vestige of her own version of morality, she
guards papers that Barclay now wants to reveal, she comments
to Barclay that 'you and Rick have destroyed each other'
(Chapter XIV). Later, full of both guilt and self-justification at
Liz's funeral, Barclay sees himself as a comic martyr, the
melodramatic version of Golding's saintly scapegoat who takes
into himself the sins of being human. His clown-like trousers
slipping down, as they had in the scene where he first shot
Tucker, Barclay tells the Church of England vicar that: 'You
will find this difficult to believe but I suffer with the stigmata.
Yes. Four of the five wounds of Christ. Four down and one to
go. No. You can't see the wounds. . . . But I assure you my
hands and feet hurt like hell – or should I say heaven?' The
vicar responds that 'You must be very proud of them' (Chapter
XVI). Tucker and Barclay are still locked in the constant
symbiotic struggle to combine and break away. They attack
each other's paper, each other's defences, and each other's
gestures toward accommodation and forgiveness. In a nearly
final reversal, Barclay decides to withhold himself and plans a
fire to burn every scrap of his paper to keep it from Tucker.
Yet, feeling mercy, he relents and claims the ground of moral
superiority. Tucker, enraged by the claim, an invasion of his
usual territory, as well as in retaliation for Barclay's shooting
him at the beginning of the novel, ends the novel by stalking,
shooting and killing Barclay. Both men are in hell, the hell they
have created with and through each other, the writer's hell that
is expressed, articulated, documented in paper and damned.
The question of Barclay's possible 'greatness' is never
approached, for he is seen only as a popular writer with no
mention of the value or substance of his fiction. The elimination
of any treatment of 'higher' art or imagination, of any judgement
that distinguishes one fiction from another, forces the novel into
the mould of the extravagantly fallible nature of all writers. Yet
the strangely comic versions and symbols, the outrageous and
incongruous echoes of traditional meaning, indicate that mutual
damnation of both writers is not the only point of Golding's
fiction. Some strange yet forceful incoherence, some echo of
universal feeling and connection to others, lies deeper in the

human psyche than damnaton, deeper than the flawed and sinful human effort to individuate. Yet this positive or communal feeling is never made clear, never given focus or the capacity to resolve any of the damnable issues of human experience, an unwillingness or inadequacy that, as Golding sees it, is perhaps the most searing damnation of paper men. Golding has, in a way, as Barclay once threatened to do, disappeared inside his own fiction and his own damnation.

The difficulty with *The Paper Men* is not that it reveals an authorial simplicity or defensiveness as some of the more literal-minded initial readers and reviewers have charged. Rather, the difficulty is inherent in the method, in the overwhelming negativity of the approach, which can create problems of focus for a reader trying to get beyond the initial problems that are reversed and reversed again. The problem is not Golding's identification with his subject but his comic remoteness from it. Yet Golding's prose itself, in its variety and impact, expresses considerable individuality and a powerful appeal. Many of his descriptions of costume or human behaviour, no matter what their moral or judgemental implications, convey an astonishingly strong appeal to the physicality and immediacy of experience. Readers can, and probably should, derive an abstract point, but the experience itself, the character's connection with or retreat from another, or the account of some conventional fad, is never abstracted or attenuated. The prose contains splendid pieces, striking metaphors or comic scenes. The absence of Halliday, regarded as more powerful and more in control of the universe the more he does not appear in expected contexts, is frequently made very funny, as are Barclay's derisive applications of various seductive machinations to the silent, virtually comatose Mary Lou. A friend of Barclay's, a homosexual reporter he encounters on his travels through the Greek Islands, is given comic lines that invert conventional literary judgements and canons, both the Classical and those in English literature. As an example of 'literary masturbation', the reporter quotes Keats's *Lamia* to show the poet a 'silly vulgarian', trying to 'proclaim . . . *complete* heterosexuality' and deserving the reductive designation of a member of the 'Cockney School' (Chapter X). Other passages are more evocative, physical and powerful in ways that resemble those in the earlier novels. At one point, on a rocky, volcanic island, Barclay visits the ruin of

what had been a cathedral, looking at the mosaics. A chip from
one of the mosaics falls to the ground:

> That tiny fragment of dirty blue stone fell a yard in front of
> me and I stood on my right foot, about to put the left one
> down but I kept it there in the air and looked at the stone. It
> was less than half an inch square. It lay directly in front of
> me. I put down my left foot and stood. Mountains throw
> cannon balls at me, churches drop a bit of stone the size of a
> finger nail . . . . there was something about that cathedral,
> an atmosphere. It was, now I saw in the absence of sunglasses,
> still darker than it had any right to be, seeing that the sun
> was brassy outside and most of the windows stark plain. You
> could call it a complete absence of gentle Jesus meek and
> mild. I didn't like it.

Yet, in the isolation and semi-darkness, with the single stone
and the bits of jewel from 'a solid silver statue of Christ' that
looks archaic, Barclay has a genuine religious experience:

> I stood there with my mouth open and the flesh crawling
> over my body. I knew in one destroying instant that all my
> adult life I had believed in God and this knowledge was a
> vision of God. Fright entered the very marrow of my bones.
> Surrounded, swamped, confounded, all but destroyed, adrift
> in the universal intolerance, mouth open, screaming, bepissed
> and beshitten, I knew my maker and I fell down. (Chapter
> XI)

Other images, like Barclay depicting himself as a crab or a
lobster, the creature with the carapace of the crustacean, yet
with worms crawling through or eating the flesh within, echo
directly some of the images built into a more consistently
patterned structure in *Pincher Martin*.

These effective bits of writing, however, always centre on
ideas and states of emotion or being rather than on characters
or relationships. Golding is still more at ease in the world of his
own imagination than in reporting or in giving an imaginative
account of what others are like and how they react. As Golding
has Barclay say of a minor character, a lawyer he encounters in
Zurich:

I remember thinking it was a good job I was no longer bothering with writing beautifully a Wilfred Barclay book because she again was a real person and useless to the novelist because he cannot describe them and they do not bother to describe themselves, existing more in their silences than their speech. (Chapter XIII)

In *The Paper Men*, however, Golding's imagination does not cohere as it does in the most deeply cogent and searching of the earlier novels, in *Pincher Martin* or *The Spire*. The particular bits of striking and sometimes brilliant comedy or metaphor are strung on a narrative structure of inchoate episodes or outrageous farce. The issues of man and his fictionalising are never resolved. The writer, like all men, is fallible, untrustworthy, always seeking to be loved in his particular uniqueness rather than as part of a larger, more generous human nature. But, beyond this, Golding makes no statement about the possibilities of human redemption or reclamation, earned or granted, not even a statement of some semi-resolution through the process of fiction itself. Golding is the writer, able to crystallise and convey certain phenomena with words, and he can sometimes do this brilliantly. He is steadfastly not more than the writer, not the God or seer, not able to provide a pattern or coherence of meaning that his fictional novelist cannot see. Although Golding's perspective is not Barclay's, and the author often judges his novelist harshly, he does not establish an authorial voice as something above Barclay, something able to see or suggest a pattern or meaning in the act of writing that the character is unable to see. The writer is mortal and flawed, like other men, with intimations of something beyond mortality that he cannot translate into meaning or pattern. Even his art provides no resolution, no version of the frequent twentieth-century literary theme that art itself can fabricate a coherence that substitutes for a God or meaning in which we can no longer believe.

The Paper Men, although less metaphorically coherent and less confident than the earlier novels as an artistic statement, is finally a humble novel about writing because it never arrogates to itself the certainty of the message about the nature of literature or fiction. In so far as it might be read as Golding's inferential statement about his career as a writer, the novelist's perspective is not at all that of the older, crusty, intemperate, paranoid, successful novelist it may appear to be on the surface. Rather, *The Paper Men* reveals the self-questioning novelist, aware of the ludicrous and the contradictory, wondering if, apart from some striking phrases and metaphors, some bits of brilliance that do not cohere, he has finally made any statement or provided any significance at all. The perspective toward the career returns to what Golding has often articulated about his early published poetry: some fine and beautiful lines, some dramatic and resonant metaphors, which may well be all the human writer can accomplish. For Golding, through his fiction and in fact, many of the metaphors, particularly those that seem to embody the whole concept of the novel, are themselves a considerable literary accomplishment in a context that questions the permanence and value of any human or literary activity.

7

Popular and Critical Reception

Although a writer's popular reputation is separable from the critical assessment of his achievement, particularly as the latter changes and develops through time, both kinds of reception are relevant in considering fiction that, like Golding's, is simultaneously difficult and involving. Thoughtful and discerning critical judgement can lead to a fuller understanding both of individual novels and of the changes visible over a whole career. The phenomenon of popularity and possible reasons for it also require treatment, both as an indication of what within Golding's fiction generates such wide and strong reponse and as a potentially interesting statement about the literate culture at a particular point in history. Serious and complicated as he is in presenting his versions of human experience, Golding has never scorned or dismissed the element of popularity among the generally literate. In addition, critics are also readers within a particular cultural setting and ordinary readers can be thoughtfully critical. The categories of response, distinguishable at their extremes, often, partially and in practice, impinge on one another.

The initial reviews of *Lord of the Flies*, like initial reviews of many innovative novels, were generally tepid and non-committal. Although almost all praised Golding's fine writing, most were hesitant about considering the implications of the metaphor of the boys on the island. They generally thought the metaphor too neat, too explicit, too heavy, or too limited – in one way or another, inadequate to suggest anything important or interesting about contemporary British society or the human condition. In the literary world of 1954, in which reviewers were still looking for new novels that might make

significant statements about post-war British society and in
which what were perceived as literary shortcomings were still
granted the apologetic explanation of fatigue after the long
years of war and austerity, no one proclaimed Golding's first
novel a particularly revealing or searching achievement. Walter
Allen, for example, found the 'children's crosses . . . too
unnaturally heavy' to allow one to 'draw conclusions' and the
novel 'however skilfully told, only a rather unpleasant and too-
easily affecting story'.[49] Several other reviewers compared the
novel to Richard Hughes's 1929 novel, *A High Wind in Jamaica*,
as a study of the savagery inherent in children, a counter to the
Victorian sentimentality of childhood innocence. Those who
made the comparison, almost without exception, saw Golding's
version as much less psychologically accurate or penetrating
and implicitly much less humane than Hughes's. The novel
was not widely noticed and achieved only moderately respectable
sales in 1954, certainly nothing close to the popularity of
Kingsley Amis's *Lucky Jim*, a first novel published during the
same year. Amis's comic mimicry and apparent iconoclasm
seemed much more the voice of a newly emerging generation in
Britain.

As *The Inheritors* and *Pincher Martin*, in 1955 and 1956, followed
Lord of the Flies, reviewers and essayists began to pay more
attention to Golding and to speculate about what might be
behind his tersely and effectively written fictions. Summarising
a series of current novels from London for *Kenyon Review* in
1957, Wayland Young called attention to Golding's frequent
use of religious symbols in *Lord of the Flies* and elsewhere,
'though the specifically Christian element in Golding's work is
always subordinate to a generalized sense of natural religion'.[50]
Others were less impressed with the significance of Golding's
metaphors. V. S. Pritchett thought Golding's 'romances', his
departures from the quotidian, rather remote and unconvincing
although well-written. He regarded *Lord of the Flies* as the most
effective of the three then published, asserting that, for all three
alike, 'Pain is the essence of Mr. Golding's subject'. Although
his use of 'pain' is close to Golding's later application of the
word 'grief', the focus on the emotional state, Pritchett also
thought that 'The idea is irrelevant'.[51] Some derogated Golding
even further. Martin Green, aware of the growing vogue for
Golding by the time he wrote his essay called 'Distaste for the

Contemporary' in *The Nation* in 1960, thought Golding pretentious and old-fashioned. Although he praised the 'discipline' of Golding's prose, he, unlike almost all other critics, asserted: 'There is not life in his language; it is all ingenuity, intention, and synthetics.' Green claimed Golding had no voice of his own, that his handling of ideas was 'too predictable, too exaggerated . . . nothing new'.[52] To a fairly considerable extent, early critical appraisals of Golding were likely to be conditioned or at least influenced by the critic's willingness, or lack of it, to endorse or follow Golding's religious perspective. This sense of shared belief crystallising literary judgement can perhaps best be illustrated by the polarity between two more sweeping generalisatons delivered in 1964 when *The Spire* appeared. David Lodge concluded that 'No English novelist of his generation has dared – and achieved – as much'. V. S. Pritchett, still gently sceptical, advised 'Better to get back to humanism'.[53] Whatever the reviews or the journalistic polarities, the popular admiration for Golding continued to grow during the late 1950s and early 1960s. Extending from the young to the wider public, particularly visible on college campuses and among recent graduates, this interest in Golding did not generally seem dependent on any sense of shared religious belief. Although Golding was not regarded as articulating any doctrine or statement about the modern world, the implications of his metaphors were often felt as requiring no explanation and as uniquely applicable to contemporary experience.

One of the first critics to demonstrate a comprehensive understanding of what Golding was doing in his various fictions, of his range of and commitment to ideas as well as of the emotions he generated, was Frank Kermode. His well-known 1959 broadcast interview with Golding was often cited and reprinted. In a 1961 essay, Kermode recognised both the interpretive difficulties in Golding's work and the fact that his perspective owed little to the literary culture of the 1950s. He saw Golding creating his fictions from a knowledgeable sense of primitive myth in 'relative isolation from any mainstream of speculation', yet not in isolation at all from an observant sense of contemporary experience. Kermode argued convincingly that the emotion that generated Golding's fictions was less explicable as 'pain' or as 'grief' than as 'guilt', an emotion contingent on the constant observation that the human being is unable to measure up to his own concept of himself, that the 'pain' is less a matter of the human being as victim of something outside himself than of the human being as both victim and victimiser, the flawed consciousness of his own imagination. Man is, thus, capable of evil, of violation of himself and other human beings, and so deserves the moral judgement that can legitimately both excoriate most human beings most of the time and venerate the occasional 'saint', the saviour of the human community who is most often its scapegoat. Kermode also saw that Golding's religion was not dependent on any particular theology. Rather, in using his own versions of various myths and echoes of mystery, Classical and Christian, coherent only in naming and locating his too convenient, too simplistically treated, targets or antagonists, Golding was trying to deal with primitive human sources of religion rather than explicitly with religious doctrine or orthodoxy. And, as Kermode pointed out, Golding's own metaphors, more carefully defined and articulated in *Pincher Martin* than they had been earlier, most effectively conveyed the emotional sense of the human experience he sought.[54] Kermode was even able, in one instance, to change Golding's mind about his own work. During their broadcast, Golding, confident in his own consciousness of all the deliberate implications of his fiction, balked when Kermode cited the well-known D. H. Lawrence dictum, 'Never trust the teller, trust the tale'. Golding called it 'absolute nonsense'. But Kermode explained something of what Lawrence meant about the process of fiction deepening and transforming conscious intention, and, by 1963, Golding was able to recognise a more complicated relationship between himself as author and his material.[55] In the late 1950s, other studies of Golding's work began to link his various metaphors as cultural and historical statements suggested by his targets and by some of the other referential sources in his fiction. Ralph Freedman, for example, writing of the first three novels in 1958, said that: 'The eighteenth-century contrast of civilization and primitivism is restated in twentieth-century terms . . . Golding renders a modern interpretation of what is human which could not have been accepted twenty or thirty years ago.'[56]

At the same time, the vogue for Golding among the young in both Britain and America continued, reaching its peak during the early 1960s. At first in a kind of spontaneous group reaction, students read *Lord of the Flies* on their own; then, the novel was frequently assigned to elicit or to draw on student interest in sixth forms and introductory university classes. As one critic has stated concerning America:

> 'On the campus it was required reading for students in political science, used to illustrate the anti-pastoral, and assigned to Peace Corps volunteers to learn "about the essential conflict between man's individual well being and the rules of society"'.[57]

For many of the literate and educated young, in both Britain and America, *Lord of the Flies* seemed to become a kind of code book, generating an enthusiasm as a voice for its own generation that had been matched, or perhaps exceeded, by J. D. Salinger's *Catcher in the Rye* about a decade earlier. The Salinger novel depicted more directly and sympathetically the vulnerable voice of the rebelling adolescent, its honesty, its sensitivity, its refusal to succumb to or tolerate all the 'phoney crap' endemic in its environment, its sense that it was wiser and less pretentious than its elders, and the sweetness and humanity of its vision. The Golding was seen as the darker novel, the more sceptical about any form of humanity or sweetness and the more fundamentally penetrating in locating the 'crap' within the adolescent as well as within the adult world. For many young people, the cults of Salinger and Golding, despite numerous possible differences in definition, existed side by side, often within the same reader. For others, the Golding seemed to replace the Salinger, as if to mark off different generations among the contemporary young. To some extent, particularly in America, the vogues were further apart in time than the dates of publication, *Catcher in the Rye* in 1951 and *Lord of the Flies* in 1954, would suggest. The cult of Salinger began in America with the immediate post-war generation of young veterans and others in the late 1940s with the publication of stories like 'For Esmé With Love and Squalor', an American version of confidence in the essential sensibility of the young war-time British 'with all your faculties intact', and 'A Perfect Day for Bananafish', with its preternaturally wise youngster, and its interest in ultimate mystery, and its scepticism about conventional forms of rational coherence. In 1951, with the

publication of *Catcher in the Rye*, the cult extended to adolescents
and began immediately to cross the ocean. With stories like
'Teddy' and 'Franny', the Salinger cult continued to grow
throughout the mid and late 1950s, enclosing the variety of
several mini-generations of the family. The vogue for *Lord of the
Flies* took longer to germinate, not really beginning among the
young until the publication of the paperback edition of 1959
and using Golding's later fiction only in so far as it reflected
attention back on *Lord of the Flies*. The cult centred on the single
novel. In some senses, the vogue for Golding seemed to
represent younger siblings reacting with a harder and more
permanent sense of the human dilemma against what they saw
as the sentimentality of those just slightly older. In other senses,
the vogues co-existed. Both felt the voices of the fiction those of
an explicitly post-Second World War generation; both as
products of the atomic age were attuned to the dangers of
earlier perspectives of confidence in the capacity of human
beings to solve human problems. Both were, in different ways,
derisively sceptical about the languages and conventions of
social assurance. Both extended the scepticism to rationality in
general, moving toward an interest in mystery and religion,
although for Salinger, this was located outside the Western
tradition entirely, in Buddha and the East, whereas for Golding,
the sense of religion was primal, referentially Christian,
Classical, Egyptian and prehistoric. Both vogues gave to the
educated and literary young a sense of hearing an authentic
voice of their own, an awareness of differences in generations,
and an attack on the complacency and confidence of their
elders whom they thought had made a mess of the world.
Although the Golding seemed harder, less sentimental, and less
approbative of the eccentrically human in both individual and
social terms, the enthusiasms for Salinger and for Golding so
frequently co-existed because they were so fundamentally alike.

Social commentators about the young sometimes exaggerated
and simplified the differences between the two vogues. Most of
such British commentators represented the difference as that
between Holden Caulfield treated as an American innocent
within a 'phoney' and corrupt society and Golding's boys as a
never sentimentalised version of human corruption itself.[58] Some
American versions, however, went considerably further and
translated the two different cults into different social and

political attitudes, one replacing the other. After the Golding cult was popularly enshrined in a 1962 article in *Time* magazine, numerous essays in serious periodicals and monthlies attempted to examine its social and cultural meaning. One essay, by Francis E. Kearns, published in *America*, the official national Catholic weekly review, developed contrasting political terms for the 'conflict' between Salinger and Golding. For Kearns, Salinger was within the tradition of 'liberal humanism', a tradition of belief in progress and reform that had begun with the governmental reforms initiated by Franklin D. Roosevelt in the 1930s, and was still visible in the 'influence' of such Presidential advisors as John Kenneth Galbraith and Arthur Schlesinger Jr (almost as if a secular WASP and a secular Jew represented contemporary forces that might divert or undercut a wise sense of the fundamental in a Roman Catholic president). Kearns called the Salinger cult 'idealistic', 'liberal' and 'romantic', contrasting it to the Golding cult that saw the human being as essentially depraved, the intellectual outgrowth of 'the Calvinist-oriented magistrates and ministers of the early Puritan establishment'. Although he thought that both traditions contained elements of human value, Kearns regarded 'liberal humanitarianism' as dominant for too long in American life and praised Golding's recognition of the evil at the centre of human experience. Kearns speculated about whether evidence of a shift toward Golding's perspective might be visible in some rightist student organisations, like Young Americans for Freedom, which welcomed books like Barry Goldwater's *The Conscience of a Conservative* and William F. Buckley's *God and Man at Yale*.[59]

Another essay, appearing just one day earlier in *Commonweal*, the weekly journal edited by Catholic laymen (each article apparently was written without knowledge of the other), by Luke M. Grande, developed the 'conflict' between Salinger and Golding in somewhat similar terms, although Grande was less specific and literal in relating the perspectives implicit in the novels to political figures or trends. Grande thought the Salinger cult, connected to other novels written just after the war, was 'characterized by a type of pessimism and spiritual fatigue that, upon rereading, seems strangely dated'. In dealing with a deeper sense of evil, and in also providing a character like Simon who grasps the 'truth', Golding, for Grande, really points toward a possible 'salvation' that appealed to contemporary youth. Grande regarded Golding as a 'genuine artist', even if 'not yet a modern Chaucer or a Dostoievski of the sixties', a writer of depth with 'more traditional humanistic concerns' than those visible in Salinger.[60] A month later, *Commonweal* published a direct exchange of opinion between Kearns and Grande, followed by further definition of their differences. They continued to argue Kearns's focus on Golding's insistence on dark human depravity versus Grande's more centrally literary and metaphorical conviction that Golding offered 'hope' for fallen man. Both, however, continued to assume social, political and religious connections between what they described as current social and political issues and the appeal of Golding to university students.[61]

Such equations of Golding's appeal with particular political figures or policies and with religious sects, which were frequent, seemed misleading and overstated, even at the time, from the point of view of many of those on American campuses. Most of the students who enthusiastically read Golding, like most of those who had consumed Salinger, had no particular political, party, sectarian or doctrinal commitments, were likely to identify themselves more with a vague literary scepticism about all practical politics or sects than with any programme. Young Americans for Freedom was minute and virtually invisible on campuses in the early 1960s, a more noteworthy presence in the encouragement it received from older and established conservatives than in anything it thought or did on the campus itself. To that extent, its relatively few members were generally more interested in contacts within established political circles and in possible future jobs than in reading anything at all. Golding also had some appeal among the growing and radical Students for a Democratic Society, which began in 1962, although the organisation did not achieve large numbers of adherents until the massive protests against racial discrimination and the war in Vietnam a few years later. Some of those among the radical students who venerated Golding saw him as harder, less sentimental, than Salinger, offering a more appropriate recognition of human depravity and thereby sanctioning all the social and political activity necessary. Golding's novels also assumed values of community and concern for others that, if translatable into politics at all, were closer to at least the abstract aims of the New Left than to any programme of the few and minute politically conservative groups. Although the kind of direct and literal political application of Golding's appeal that writers like Kearns, Grande and the editors of *Time* magazine postulate simplifies and distorts the literary culture, something in Golding's appeal for the young (and for many of those who taught the young – sometimes those two populations are difficult to separate) in both Britain and American could be called culturally although not politically conservative. Oldsey and Weintraub, critics and university teachers, publishing their book on Golding in both Britain and America in 1965, discussed Golding as appealing as an iconoclast operating in opposition to a liberal or self-exploratory literary tradition:

> Put another way, *he is a reactionary in the most basic sense of the word*. Reacting strongly to certain disagreeable aspects of life and literature as he sees them, he writes with a revolutionary heat that is contained rather than exploded within his compressed style. Restoration rather than preservation is his aim: he would restore concepts of Belief, Free Will, Individual Responsibility, Sin, Forgiveness (or Atonement, anyway), Vision, and Divine Grace. He would restore principles in an unprincipled world; he would restore belief to a world of willful unbelievers. . . . It might not be the voice of a Dostoevsky or Melville or Conrad or Camus, but certainly it was not the voice of still another angry young man. With each successive novel Golding seemed to be marking an end to all that – the novel of manners, the novel of social commentary – and thus to the great tradition as well. It was as though he were pointing at *Howard's End* as a literary cul-de-sac.[62]

Although this depiction of the cultural 'reactionary' carries some credibility, the lines of its reasoning become increasingly tenuous in the excessive specification. Much more vaguely expressed, Golding's appeal to the young, especially strong in the early 1960s, owed far more to feelings that he depicted something hard, intractable, permanent and essential about human beings and their connections with others than it did to any of the stretched links of social or political interpretation.

Given the combination of Golding's strong, direct, immediate emotional or visceral appeal and the difficulty or ambiguity of his content, much of the literary criticism during the decade following the appearance of *Lord of the Flies* concentrated on the structure of his fiction. In the work of so consciously compressed a writer, structure seemed to provide a shape or an order through which to describe the intensity that doctrine or argument could not approach. John Peter, in 1957, was the first to apply the term 'fable' to Golding's fiction. Almost as soon, however, as Peter had defined the term, he (slightly) and others (more centrally) began to question how fully or centrally it applied. In the sense that the message of the fable seems implicit all along, that the events move toward some moral shape pre-ordained, most critics would agree that Golding wrote fables. But, almost immediately, critics began to point out, Golding's structures often involved some sort of switch at the end – the apparent rescue in *Lord of the Flies*, the change to the perspective of *homo sapiens* in *The Inheritors*, the realisation that Pincher Martin has been dead all along – that leads a reader to question the comprehensiveness of fabulistic structure, or to wonder whether the moral implications of the unexpected switch reversed or intensified the moral implications of the fable itself that had been visible from the beginning. Golding had referred to his endings as 'gimmicks', and he was sometimes taken more literally at his self-deflating word than a fuller reading of the novels would warrant. John Whitley, publishing a book on *Lord of the Flies* in 1970, provided the most comprehensive account of both the moral and structural implications of Golding's first fable, but he also wondered explicitly how thoroughly and intrinsically the associations of the term applied.[63] In first proposing 'fable', John Peter had been less certain that it worked for the densely packed and difficult metaphor of *Pincher Martin* than for the two earlier novels. Other critics, like Margaret Walters and Howard Babb, whose idea of the 'fable' sometimes required the conflation of structural endings and statements about whether or not hope for human salvation existed, focused on *Pincher Martin* as the test case for the application of 'fable' to Golding's fictional structures. Golding himself acknowledged that here, if anywhere, the charge of 'gimmickry' had some justice.[64] His own subsequent explanations of the novel, his sense of what he meant the novel to suggest, rely far less on narrative and structure than they do on all the metaphysical implications of the metaphor itself. Some critics stretched definitions and implications of 'fable' to include the novel; others acknowledged that the term was becoming less useful as a way to explain centrally what Golding was doing. Gradually, as critical accounts of Golding's increasing canon became more knowledgeable and sophisticated, the use of 'fable' largely faded from discussion. Don Crompton, for example, in the best recent critical work on Golding, published in 1985, wrote that initially the ending of *Pincher Martin* seemed a 'cheap' theatrical trick, 'its only purpose was to alert the imperceptive reader to the true nature of Pincher Martin's plight'. But, Crompton continued, the later and wiser Golding would have recognised that the 'true ending' of the book was in the image of ragged claws occurring some pages earlier, 'the poetic resolution of the book', and would have cut those final pages. He would instinctively have known that the 'complexity and subtlety' of his concept were 'too great for the tightly controlled and ordered structure he had imposed on it'.[65] As Crompton indicated, Golding, especially at the beginning of his literary career, deliberately isolated from other writers, had not a very sure sense of his audience or of how much he needed to write in order to be clear. He tended to overexplain in some ways, underexplain in others. After *Pincher Martin*, however, Golding, perhaps more sensitive to the ways in which readers and critics interpret, confuse and conflate the implications of literary form, did not make his changes, questions or underlinings quite so obtrusive. Nor did he rely on structure, on the 'fable', to carry quite so much of his fictional message.

A great deal of the early criticism, confronting all the difficulties in understanding Golding's world, spent considerable time in uncovering sources and parallels in earlier literature. One of the unquestionable sources for Golding's fiction has been the literature of the ancient Greeks in which he has always been saturated. His occasional reviews in the early 1960s, like one of Robert Fitzgerald's 1962 translation of *The Odyssey*, demonstrate Golding's wide knowledge and firmly confident judgement about the Classics. From the beginning, critics have found sources among Greek literature and myths for many of the elements in Golding's fiction. Peter Green, for example, in 1963, thought the defeats of man's rational attempts to survive in all the early novels treatments of the Prometheus myth, and *Pincher Martin*, in its establishment of the rock as 'purgatorial', an 'Aeschylean novel'.[66] The most thorough treatment of Golding's Greek sources is in Bernard Dick's book, published in 1967. Jocelin in *The Spire* is connected with Oedipus, and Dick claims that the novel is 'the most perfect evocation of Classical Tragedy in our era'.[67] Dick also asserts that Golding's method, his use of a particular work as a target or as a model to change or incorporate into his own fiction is itself classical in locus, the whole process of the myths receiving successive and different representations in a tradition of fictionalising. Others have extended the influence of ancient myth in Golding, as in a long discussion in Crompton's book in which he connects a number of the characters in *The Spire* with figures in ancient Norse myths.[68] On the whole, Golding has not objected to others finding sources for his work in classical or other ancient traditions of literature and legend. In 1970, he acknowledged the influences of Greek drama and myth, particularly the Promethean, and stated that 'I think it is true that Greek literature really has been the *big* literary influence in my life, but I think that that may very well have come to an end, and so may I.'[69] Without quite so definitive a conclusion, Golding's recent work has had less classical influence, at least less in total structure or through some central myth. Occasional references are still embedded in his prose.

Golding has, however, been less tolerant of critical source-hunting in literature and ideas other than the Classical or legendary. He often uses essays to try to set the record straight, and he is comically referring to the location of his fiction in random and eccentric places when he states, in 1976, that 'I am the raw material of an academic light industry', 'a moving target'.[70] The closer to the contemporary the source, the more likely Golding is either to object or to retreat into a deferential and uncommitted silence. He once wrote of how he enjoyed giving a lecture on his first visit to America until he discovered that the lecture was being taped by someone not involved actively in the discussion, yielding 'a fossilized impression of my social footprints'.[71] It is as if, for Golding, what is more recent, including his own work, is more transitory and accidental. Only the time-tested and the Classics deserve the firmness of commitment and conscious influence that an acknowledgement of sources implies. Golding has been particularly sceptical with regard to a number of essays trying to demonstrate the influence of Freudian theory on *Lord of the Flies*. For various writers, Ralph was an 'id', Piggy an 'ego', and Simon a 'superego', or for others, Jack the troublesome and ungovernable 'id'. Other critics talked of the ritual of killing the pig as a Freudian version of an Oedipal wedding night ceremony. Some critics, more restrained, like John Whitley, have traced Golding's Freudianism more vaguely through the intermediary of Richard Hughes, whose *High Wind in Jamaica* draws explicitly on Freud's theories of childhood and infant sexuality.[72] Golding has not apparently commented on the influence of Hughes, but he has been directly derogatory about any suggestions of Freudian influence. After recounting some of the Freudian suggestions, deliberately vague about the application of the terms, Golding concluded: 'And to think I've never read Freud in my life'.[73]

Golding has tried, quite consciously, to insulate his fiction from some of those sources most generally regarded as intellectually seminal for the contemporary literary consciousness. Bernard Dick, the critic who has treated Golding's ancient Greek sources most exhaustively, asserted metaphorically in his preface that: 'Sigmund Freud, Franz Kafka, Jean-Paul Sartre, and even Joseph Conrad are absent from the Golding bookcase.'[74] One might add that Golding would expunge any taint of Marx or hints of existential thought. Although such statements and those of Golding himself may well be true in terms of conscious or direct borrowing, influence, for a person as literate, thoughtful and involved with ideas as Golding is, is a much more indirect and complicated issue. Granted the conscious and safely documentable influences are Classical, but Golding's work also seems to reveal smatterings of disseminated and indirect influences from modern culture. William Nelson, the editor of the first source book on *Lord of the Flies*, was not wrong to include, along with a full selection of criticism available in 1963, selections he called 'Related Readings' from the works of Ballantyne, Thomas Hobbes, Jean Jacques Rousseau, Freud, Jung, modern anthropologists like Sir James George Frazer, Joseph Campbell and Ashley Montague, and contemporary religious thinkers like Henry Bamford Parkes and Burnet Easton. Among twentieth-century novelists, Conrad's speculations on the consequences of civilisation seem to echo throughout the fiction. Direct influence is less the point than connections or reversals that the ideas may suggest in the minds of readers trying to work out their intellectual responses to Golding's difficult fiction.

The difficulties, however, have led some critics to strain for parallels that, although potentially interesting, seem merely superficial resemblances or are forced to carry more critical weight than they can bear. While seldom trying to demonstrate actual influence on Golding, and thus not easy to dismiss unequivocally, some early Golding critics suggested numerous resemblances or parallels that now, with greater knowledge and more thought, seem to strain credibility. Oldsey and Weintraub, although cogent in their scepticism about the influence of Freud or the applicability of Freudian diagrams of consciousness to *Lord of the Flies*, often developed parallels so explicitly and heavily that they became questionable rather than suggestive. Although Golding's imagination sometimes has the edge of a scathing Swiftian tone, Oldsey and Weintraub labelled Golding's 'key source of inspiration' Swift's perspective in *Gulliver's Travels*[75] and connected some of the place names on Pincher Martin's rock to the two London Underground lines necessary to string them together as stations, whereas the final episode in the novel was linked definitively to the model of Conrad's fiction as an illustration of multiple narration. Golding's *Free Fall* was an extended response to Camus' *The Fall*. Jocelin, in *The Spire*, in long explanatory passages, was connected with both Ibsen's master builder and Browning's bishop ordering his tomb at St Praxed's. The authors followed Martin Green in reading Golding's general attitude as a possible rejection of science linked culturally with the phenomenon C. P. Snow complained of among literary intellectuals. Bernard Dick, generally far more contained by the Classical in his texture of relevant literary reference, also made the connection with Snow, reading the polarity Golding established between Rowena Pringle and Nick Shales in *Free Fall* as if it were a counter in the Leavis–Snow public controversy about the cultures of the humanities and science. Other critics established vaguer and more general parallels, like Howard Babb's link between Golding and Hardy as novelists possessed by their themes, relentlessly exploring the condition of man as they see it, however differently they evaluate that condition. And both of them leave one with an impression of singular honesty, for they hold fast to their essential visions of man and refuse to compromise with beliefs and attitudes more conventional at the time of their writing.[76]

An unexceptionable parallel, but not one that is sufficiently exclusive or discriminating to be critically useful. Many such parallels seemed interesting in the context of first reading a difficult and densely textured novelist whose references and saturation with the literary and mythical past invited speculation. But the parallels, when inspected, were often too specific or too vague, yielded less than they seemed to promise, and deflected attention from a centre that was uniquely the perspective of William Golding.

Much of this forced 'academic light industry' in these relatively early critical accounts of Golding's fiction involved enthusiastic and sometimes undifferentiated searches for meaning and connection that helped to stimulate serious critical interest in Golding. Yet the soundest and most comprehensive early critical book on Golding, that written by Mark Kinkead-Weekes and Ian Gregor and first published in 1967, generally avoided tracking possible literary sources. Kinkead-Weekes and Gregor recognised at the outset that *Lord of the Flies* had become so widely popular because it seemed to combine 'narrative momentum and thematic clarity' which later, 'greater Golding novels have failed to achieve'.[77] The later novels, particularly *Pincher Martin* and *The Spire*, were 'greater' because finally more ambiguous, less amenable to explanatory categories like 'fable'. At its best, Golding's work resembled sculpture, the individual novels illustrating a tension between the form and Golding's imagination that moved toward the creation of significant cultural myth. Yet Golding's kind of myth could not easily be crystallised since it was concerned with 'modes of imagination, not philosophical views'.[78] Golding had, successively, penetrated more and more deeply into the imaginative terrain of culturally significant myth as he successively disengaged his perspective from the simplicities of fable. Most more recent critics, like Arnold Johnston, have similarly valued Golding's complex and mythic intensity more highly than the earlier works that more

closely resemble fables. A few critics, like Leighton Hodson in
1969, seemed to lament the fact that Golding had 'lost . . . a
truly popular following' because of increasing 'technical
complexity'.[79] Most, however, recognised that some differences
between popular and critical response were inevitable as
Golding probed his unique imagination more deeply in his
fiction. While *Lord of the Flies* continued to be the only novel
that generated widespread popular interest and commitment,
The Spire, both when it was published in 1964 and frequently in
the years since, was hailed by both reviewers and critics as
Golding's finest achievement.

With the publication of *The Pyramid* in 1967, a fiction centrally
locatable in social and historical time and space, Golding was
widely recognised to have changed his imaginative focus.
Although some welcomed what they saw as Golding credibly
demystifying himself and his fictions, many critics thought
Golding less good, less searching and distinctive, when setting
his metaphors for human experience within a knowable social
world. This point of view had been articulated earlier in the
response to *Free Fall*, the only one of the first five novels to use a
setting with conventional boundaries for both space and time.
Kinkead-Weekes and Gregor, for example, in an article written
in 1960, well before the publication of their book or *The Pyramid*,
had recorded their disappointment with *Free Fall*, believing, as
did a number of other critics, that Golding was less interesting
and unique when dealing with human experience in more
familiar settings.[80] The setting, however, was not the only issue
in discussion of *The Pyramid*. As Howard Babb, writing in 1970,
pointed out, *The Pyramid* was like *Free Fall* in setting and in
being less held in by a rigid pattern than the other novels were,
but *The Pyramid* was different in depicting a greater sense of the
influence of the environment and a greater consciousness of
people other than or different from the focus of the narrative.
Most critics since have acknowledged this difference, as they
have acknowledged the gradual loosening of Golding's forms.
Among critics writing in the 1980s, almost all see Golding's
gradual loosening of form beginning in *Free Fall*, followed by his
most significant achievement in brilliantly combining form with
its opposite in *The Spire*. The symbol of the cathedral and its
spire, both multiform and intensely directed upward, both
contradictory in origin and constant in aspiration, is sufficiently

capacious to hold all that Golding represents about complex individual, communal and emotionally religious and cosmic experience. Critics see Golding, beginning with *The Pyramid*, moving toward a different sense of form, one much more conventional within the traditions of English fiction. Arnold Johnston, for example, in 1980, sees *The Pyramid* as impelled by something like the targets of Wells and Ballantyne for Golding's first two novels. The difference is that, for the first two, the target was an antagonist explicitly mentioned. In *The Pyramid*, Johnson argues, the other work is the model as much as the antagonist and is only implicitly connected, never mentioned although a constant presence in similarity and reference. The model is Dickens' *Great Expectations*, Oliver the Pip of a century later learning about his world through a reversal or a modification of his 'expectations'. Bounce, for example, is Miss Havisham, her ostensible lessons rejected and her genuine lessons, emerging from the pain of her own thwarted experience, seen by the young protagonist only in retrospect. Johnston develops many other parallels, some of which seem central, some trivial, and Crompton is perhaps on more secure ground critically in limiting the specific connection with *Great Expectations* to the last of the three episodes in *The Pyramid*. Whatever one's response to the importance of the particular parallel, *The Pyramid* does show Golding following some of the more conventional functions of the nineteenth- and twentieth-century English novel, the individual character finding his or her identity both through and in rebellion from the surrounding environment.

Neither critics nor the public demonstrated much interest when Golding published *The Scorpion God* in 1971. The fiction set in Egypt, like Golding's plays, has never generated much enthusiasm or attention. In part, the judgement is literary in that the work, although done deftly, is farcical or superficial, or both, and operates on a level of consciousness much less involving than do the metaphors that are the major novels. But the setting itself may also have something to do with the general lack of deep and literate interest in Golding's Egypt. In a way, Egypt itself represents the antagonistic form, an attraction initially generated for Golding by its difference from the more usual forms of traditional and historical location. In that it never develops beyond an antagonism, an iconoclastic thorn in the side of the dominant culture, the sense of Egypt remains shallow. Golding is, however, not alone in his effort to make the Egyptian past more centrally part of the tradition of modern man. Two ambitious, thoughtful and talented novelists, both just slightly younger than Golding, have in recent years made roughly similar attempts. John Fowles in *Daniel Martin* and Norman Mailer in *Ancient Evenings* have both tried to represent the history of contemporary man as significantly connected to Egyptian civilisation and myth. Yet neither novel has been granted, by critics or by the public, the kind of enthusiasm and cultural assent that each author has been granted willingly for fictions locating the modern consciousness among more familiar spaces in history. Whether these novels are all particular failures or whether the literate culture is generally unable or unwilling to stretch itself to the significance of Egypt is difficult to distinguish. But, for Golding, as for others, the Egyptian locus has never created the enthusiasm or the emotions that suggest profundity which his other fictions, his historical, Christian and Classical metaphors, have generated with such startling force.

After 1971, Golding published no fiction for eight years and seemed quietly suspended at the edge of general literary consciousness. Although he gave occasional talks, they received little notice. At the same time, little critical material about Golding was published during most of the 1970s, as if critics were biding time in much the same way the writer was. The only notable critical exception is a 1974 book by Virginia Tiger, exploring more fully the complicated structural patterns of the novels to achieve a complex, often paradoxical, view of human experience. When *Darkness Visible* appeared in 1979, critics and reviewers praised it as an ambiguous, all-inclusive attempt at cultural vision, as if Golding had finally assembled the visionary elements of all his earlier fiction to create the comprehensive cultural statement he had hitherto only suggested. Critics conveyed a sense of Golding achieving something of his own 'expectations' in terms that were literary, historical and religious, although without the remoteness or the triviality of the Egyptian mode. Golding's 'saint' had finally become his central character, and the issues were dramatised in terms of the English cultural history of several generations. Similarly, *Rites of Passage* earned critical favour as dealing significantly with both the nature of art and a central cultural and historical conflict. It won a prestigious prize. But neither novel was a great popular success or achieved much of a cult following. Golding did not seem to speak for anyone other than himself, although almost all who discussed him acknowledged that he spoke for himself and his mysteries with great clarity and force. He was seen as creating individualistic, rather quirky, religious visions of his worlds, both contemporary and historical. These were regarded as profound and complex statements about those worlds, not easy to categorise and never sufficiently explained either by structural patterns or by reference to Golding's commentary on some element in the exterior contemporary world. Critics and reviewers, no matter how they might separate themselves from the author through minor individual reservation, accorded Golding the respect of recognising the personal, social and religious visions he had transformed into art.

Recent serious criticism of Golding's earlier fiction has been influenced by the resurgence of interest in *Darkness Visible* and *Rites of Passage*, and has consequently been both understanding and appreciative. Critics have concentrated on the centrally religious vision of Golding's imagination, seeing the moral assertions and the social commentary as a way into the more difficult, mysterious and profound statements about the nature of the human being and his connections, or lack of them, to a world beyond him. Don Crompton's book (published in 1985, although Crompton died in 1983 and the book was completed by Julia Briggs) locates a significant change in Golding's work in *The Spire*, calling it 'the first book of his later phase'. For Crompton, *The Spire* passes beyond the 'technical perfection' and the 'defined areas of conflict' of the earlier novels to greater mysteries, uncertainties and a 'sense of cosmic significance'. The novel is 'about the inextricable mixture of faith, folly, arrogance, and submitted desire that makes every work of art at once a miracle and a self-betrayal'.[81] Others, too, see *The Spire* as Golding's most complex, visionary metaphor, brilliant in an intricate process of both reference and condensation that had begun in *Pincher Martin* but was extended considerably in *The Spire*. Jocelin, too, is seen as a fully tragic figure, not just tragic through references to the Greek or to early pre-Christian man, but developed carefully into a model of the classically tragic through both the complicated characterisation of his flawed and aspiring nature and the metaphorical course of events that lead him through significant self-discovery and revelation.[82] Jocelin is Golding's fullest depiction of representative man from the point of view of religious possibility. Recognition of this and its implications in Golding criticism generally has also been helped by the publication of some of Golding's own remarks and essays, as his delivery, in a talk in 1976, of what he claimed had originally been a 'prelude' to *The Spire* that he had decided not to publish with the novel. The 'prelude' announces the clear intention to add the 'spire' and all it symbolised to Trollope's otherwise admirable depiction of the whole range of society represented by Barchester.[83] Golding saw himself, as have most of his recent sensitive readers, as getting beyond the distractions of particular or contemporary societies to the fundamental nature of man both within and apart from human society. Only after having achieved his statement symbolically in *The Spire* did Golding attempt to detail more carefully and copiously what the surrounding society was. For more recent admirers of Golding, whatever the quality of his various adumbrations of history and society since, he has never lost the searching, cogent, implicitly tragic sense of what the human being both is and might be that he so forcefully dramatised in *The Spire*.

Golding's re-emergence as a public figure following the publication of *Darkness Visible* and *Rites of Passage* led to more articles of journalistic appraisal and requests for interviews than he had received in almost twenty years. Perhaps this climate, the questions about what kinds of statement about contemporary man his works presented or represented and the responses that were generally less defensive and obfuscatory than they had sometimes been during his great popularity in the early 1960s led to the award of the Nobel Prize in 1983, granted specifically for his essays published as *A Moving Target*. But, at least for those who write in English, the award of the Nobel Prize has sometimes been a sword of honour double-edged in that it seldom has been universally acclaimed. The moment a writer is so singled out, critics and journalists find reasons why he or she deserved it less than did another writer ignored. This reaction is certainly understandable in respect to a tradition in which James Joyce, Virginia Woolf, Arnold Bennett, Henry James and Thomas Hardy did not win Novel Prizes, while Rudyard Kipling, John Galsworthy, Sinclair Lewis and Pearl Buck did. Similarly, in more recent years, the Nobel Prizes awarded to John Steinbeck, Saul Bellow, I. B. Singer and Golding have been publicly questioned, particularly in view of the fact that writers such as Borges, Navokov and Anthony Powell have not received the honour. Commentators derogate the Nobel itself in the name of a higher conception of art, an argument that has some force when applied to selections like Pearl Buck and I. B. Singer, less when applied to the others. Journalists then speculate about the kinds of social commentary or vision that may be requisite criteria for Nobel selection, or, sometimes, that Nobel selection itself is the imprimatur of not quite first-rate art. In the selection of Golding, even one of the judges of the Swedish Academy itself publicly dissented from the majority decision, announcing that he did not think Golding deserved the honour. A number of others followed his judgement and, like similar arguments going back for more than half a century, complained that the criteria of the Swedish Academy had more to do with the propulsion of respectable social or historical visions than it did with art, technique or the avant-garde. Some of these attitudes, particularly those stigmatising Golding as an antiquated and visionary poseur far from either a literary perspective central to the culture or an emerging and definable avant-garde, were repeated and intensified in the reviews of Golding's next novel, *The Paper Men*. The character of Barclay was discussed as if it was a self-portrait and reduced to crusty paranoia; the social vision, such as it is, was treated in similarly reductive and irrelevant ways. While *The Paper Men*, too much undercut by farce and the deliberately outrageous, is far from Golding's most profound vision concerning England or the nature of the writer, it deserves and doubtless will eventually be accorded more judicious and appropriate critical treatment. That treatment will certainly include the fact that it, like all Golding's novels, is centrally metaphor. In addition, for Golding, any equation constructed that connects author with central character needs to be established through and include layers of symbolic identification and separation, needs to recognise an author, never literal-minded, writing out of numerous sides of himself and his imagination that are inevitably contradictory.

Golding's own comments about his work remain cautious and humble. Less defensive or arch than he sometimes was twenty-five years ago, he still resists any tendency within or outside himself to become the contemporary oracle. As he wrote in *An Egyptian Journal*:

> There has descended on me . . . an orotundity which I have come to define as *Nobelitis*. This is a pomposity born of the fact that one is treated as representative of more than oneself by someone conscious of representing more than himself.[84]

Reviewers recognised Golding's resistance to the oracular when *An Egyptian Journal* was published in 1985. The review in *TLS*, for example, begins with the statement that none of those impressed with the significance of the culture of ancient Egypt, like Agatha Christie or Norman Mailer, have managed to translate their devotion into usable mythical terms for contempories. Yet, among these, Golding most acutely realises that a long interest in Egyptology is most likely to get in the way of both its application and any sensitive recording of contemporary Egypt. Even at that, Golding later felt the book not quite humble enough. When, in a 1985 interview, he was asked if he had missed anything in his account of his Egyptian tour that he would amend, he replied: 'I didn't insist enough on the Egyptian's perfect right to be an Egyptian and not an aging Englishman . . . in a motorboat.'[85]

The humility applies to issues other than the Egyptian, for Golding invariably backs away from any suggestions that take specific applications of his visions out of the literary and fictional forms in which he sets them. He frequently, in interviews, returns to the theme that he is a writer, that this is just fiction. Yet he remains sensitive to the possibility of transforming vision, the possibility that the human being can both accept and overcome a nature that is invariably both evil and good. If, as he has recently said, *Lord of the Flies* has 'original sin in it', 'what nobody's noticed is that it also has original virtue'.[86] His sense of religion never follows a sectarian orthodoxy and his sense of vision is invariably complex. He has said: 'I would call myself a universal pessimist but a cosmic optimist.'[87] Only metaphor, only the device singularly particular to the artist, can bring such vision with all its contradicatory implications into understandable form. Man's rational thought separates   and   distinguishes;   the   artist's   imaginative constructions, his or her metaphors, unite to depict the complexities and contradictions of experience coherently, as can the dreams or unarticulated emotional visions of readers who respond strongly to Golding. Sometimes Golding's metaphors, in their clarity and visceral appeal, seem to simplify their subjects. Sometimes, too, when the narratives become outrageous farce, the tone seems to violate the subject, the farce itself the pose of Golding's excessive humility or self-derogation. More often, however, especially in *Pincher Martin, The Spire, Darkness Visible,* and *Rites of Passage,* Golding's metaphors provide an intense and coherent shape for all the contradictory experience. Within these shapes, he is able to make moral and social judgements without committing himself to a rigorous and vulnerable moral framework. Living and writing within a culture that questions the authority of moral or social frameworks, a culture too diverse, uncertain and sensitive to all the ambiguities of experience to sanction one moral framework over another, Golding has made his metaphors the substitute for confident and extensive moral assertions, his profound and complicated searchings the substitute for doctrine. In shaping a number of these interesting and penetrating fictions, Golding has fully earned the serious attention his work has received. The literary culture is, perhaps, too occupied with 'greatness', too concerned with the attempt to distinguish the contemporary 'great' from the merely 'good', as critics sometimes debate the question about a writer still in mid-career.[88] That kind of grade-giving accolade is always arguable and finally silly. Enough to say of Golding that he has constructed a number of complicated, impacted metaphors that suggest difficult human questions and judgements, and that he has presented these in terse, involving and emotional forms, that he has in his fiction duplicated states of feeling and being. He fully deserves both reading and the public recognition that the award of the Nobel Prize suggests.

Yet something of Golding still remains on the fringes of literary discussion and concern. His work is invariably singular. One finds it difficult to imagine, even from some future retrospective point of view, talk of a Golding generation in English literature. He is immersed in literary tradition, yet he also seems to stand aside from it, not himself to illustrate some element within the tradition, some incorporation of others that changes, adapts and perhaps advances the tradition, in the way

that T. S. Eliot, for example, does. One of the closest parallels
to Golding's career, both as a writer and in terms of reputation,
may be that of Tennyson. Although such vast parallels
are always questionable, potentially suggestive rather than
demonstrable, Tennyson and Golding stand within and against
their cultures in roughly similar ways. Of course, Golding is
less a voice for the age than some thought Tennyson to be,
although this more diverse age is less one that could sanction
such a sonorous and assimilating voice. The fact that Tennyson
incorporated his legends and myths into poetry is a less
significant difference than it might seem to be, for Golding, in a
partial sense, has always remained the poet he began,
committed more to the intense evocations of particular
experiences than to the implications of his continuities of event
and narrative. In trying to explain his designation of *The Spire*
as Golding's greatest work thus far, Don Crompton talks of it
as having achieved a status Golding always 'aspired to but
never before reached', that of the extended 'dramatic poem'.[89]
Both Golding and Tennyson, at their best, achieve their most
intense passages as states of feeling, not as the conclusion of
inevitable narratives or progressions of events. Their long works
are not organised logically, not sequential statements, but are
crystallisations of emotions and states of being. While Golding's
language does not have quite the musicality of Tennyson's, it
has a similar sonority, a sense of finality, and many of his
particular passages echo a quality of Tennyson's in generating
strong feelings through intense and viscerally effective prose.

   The suggestions of similarity, in the relationship of the serious
writer to his respective literary culture, between those two
rather isolated figures born just over a century apart help to
reinforce the parallel. Golding himself has talked of the parallel
in his respect for Tennyson's 'interior stance', although 'more
rigid even than mine', and his realisation that 'like Tennyson I
lacked intellectual mobility'.[90] Both writers always seek to
express the single truth, the 'totality, God and man and
everything else that *is* in every state and level of being'[91] in a
literary culture in which most others are sceptical about or
indifferent to singularities or truths. In their constant focus on
the religious and the cosmic meaning, both Golding and
Tennyson often lose sight of people, are not generally at their
best or most cogent in characterising individuals. Opposites in

this sense would be writers like Angus Wilson, Dickens and Trollope, always most sensitive to the varieties of individual human behaviour. Golding and Tennyson, too, are both vulnerable to the criticisms of those who see literature as primarily a product of an intellectual tradition. As Golding insists that he is immune from the influence of Freudianism, Marxism, Existentialism and similar strains of thought in contemporary intellectual life, so Tennyson ignored or rejected the implications of many of the thinkers influencing his own age. That quality of Tennyson's has been strongly derogated, especially in the twentieth century when W. H. Auden, rather unfairly, could write of Tennyson: 'He had the finest ear, perhaps, of any English poet; he was also undoubtedly the stupidest.'[92] Golding, too, can seem insular in his deliberate and sometimes unknowing distance from some of the currents of contemporary thought in their intellectualised forms, can lack 'intellectual mobility'. But it is not, for either Golding or Tennyson, an issue of intelligence or of indifference to ideas. Auden's comment is undiscerning, as even a less extreme version of it would be if applied to Golding. Intellectuals within the main stream of a culture ran the risk of succumbing to one doctrine or another, of limiting or distorting themselves in allegiance to the vectors through which the literate society might see itself at a particular moment. Golding has never done this, never succumbed to intellectual fashion, and all his fictions have been the product of an individual, searching and interesting intelligence.

Both Tennyson and Golding also reveal constantly metaphorical imaginations, perspectives inevitably and almost automatically using the details of experience they observe as part of metaphorical constructions about the human condition. Their imaginations are in constant focus on what they see (and see with considerable complexity) as most profoundly central to the experience of man within the universe. Golding and Tennyson are always writers, always aware that the life they depict is within their own imaginations, is not a statement for the world, the culture, or for all literate people. Neither would add footnotes to anthologies. In this sense, in all their works, both Tennyson and Golding as writers are always cognisant that a statement embodied within the art itself is not the same as an oracular statement delivered for the world's attention. In this sense, both share an ultimate humility, a recognition of both the intense virtues and the isolated limitations of art itself. While clearly all these parallels can be pushed too far, and more differences between the two exist than have been here acknowledged, Golding holds a place in the tradition of English literature, standing somewhat to one side, like that of a contemporary Tennyson in a century much more sceptical and wary of Tennysons than even his own age had been.

Notes

1. Martin Green, 'Distaste for the Contemporary', *The Nation*, 21 May 1960. Reprinted in William Nelson, *William Golding's Lord of the Flies: A Source Book* (New York: Odyssey Press, 1963), pp. 75–82.

2. William Golding, *The Hot Gates and Other Occasional Pieces* (London: Faber and Faber, 1965), p. 168.

3. Jack I. Biles, *Talk: Conversation with William Golding* (New York: Harcourt Brace Jovanovich, 1970), p. 84.

4. Ibid., pp. 89–90.

5. Ibid., pp. 26–9.

6. Ibid., p. 33.

7. Ibid., pp. 59–63.

8. Ibid., p. 49.

9. Ibid., pp. 7–10.

10. William Golding, *A Moving Target* (London: Faber and Faber, 1982), p. 72.

11. William Golding, *An Egyptian Journal* (London and Boston: Faber and Faber, 1985), p. 207.

12. *A Moving Target*, p. 5.

13. Biles, *Talk*, pp. 96–7.

14. *A Moving Target*, pp. 22–3.

15. *The Hot Gates*, p. 19.

16. *A Moving Target*, p. 55.

17. Biles, *Talk*, pp. 79–81.

18. Ibid., p. 104.

19. Bernard S. Oldsey and Stanley Weintraub, *The Art of William Golding* (Bloomington and London: Indiana University Press, 1965), p. 172.

20. William Golding, interview with Maurice Dolbier, *New York Herald Tribune*, 20 May 1962. Quoted in Biles, *Talk*, p. 105.

21. *The Hot Gates*, p. 85.

22. William Golding and Frank Kermode, 'The Meaning of it All', broadcast on the BBC Third Programme, 28 August 1959. Transcript published in *Books and Bookmen*, October 1959.

23. Samuel Hynes, *William Golding*, Columbia Essays on Modern Writers, No. 2 (New York and London: Columbia University Press, 1964).

24. *A Moving Target*, pp. 198–9.

25. Ibid., pp. 186–7.

26. Ibid., p. 192.

27. Ibid., p. xi.

28. Ibid., p. 194.

29. Ibid., pp. 158–63.

30. Ibid., pp. 148–52.

31. Ibid., pp. 129–46.

32. William Golding, interview with Henry David Rosso, United Press International, published in *Ann Arbor News*, Ann Arbor Michigan, 5 December 1985.

33. John Peter, 'The Fables of William Golding', *Kenyon Review*, Autumn 1957. Reprinted in Nelson, *Golding's Lord of the Flies*, pp. 21–34.

34. John S. Whitley, *Golding: Lord of the Flies*, Studies in English Literature, no. 42, (London: Edward Arnold, 1970), pp. 3, 41.

35. Golding and Kermode, 'The Meaning of it All'.

36. Don Crompton, *A View from the Spire: William Golding's Later Novels*, edited and completed by Julia Briggs (Oxford: Blackwell, 1985), p. 29.

37. Oldsey and Weintraub, *Art of Golding*, p. 26.

38. See John Fowles, *Daniel Martin* (Boston: Little, Brown and Company, 1977), p. 86.

39. Crompton, *Golding: Later Novels*, pp. 61–2.

40. Biles, *Talk*, p. 3.

41. Arnold Johnston, *Of Earth and Darkness: The Novels of William Golding* (Columbia and London: University of Missouri Press, 1980), p. 98.

42. Ibid., pp. 98–9.

43. Crompton, *Golding's Later Novels*, p. 96.

44. Biles, *Talk*, p. 16.

45. *A Moving Target*, p. 172.

46. Crompton, *Golding's Later Novels*, pp. 135–6.

47. *A Moving Target*, pp. 125–6.

48. Crompton, *Golding's Later Novels*, p. 165.

49. Walter Allen, 'New Novels', *New Statesman*, 25 September 1954. Reprinted in Nelson, *Golding's Lord of the Flies*, p.3.

50. Wayland Young, 'Letter from London', *Kenyon Review*, Summer, 1957. Reprinted in Nelson, *Golding's Lord of the Flies*, pp. 18–21.

51. V. S. Pritchett, 'Secret Parables', *New Statesman*, 2 August 1958. Reprinted in Nelson, *Golding's Lord of the Flies*, pp. 35–9.

52. Green, 'Distaste for the Contemporary', pp. 79–81.

53. Oldsey and Weintraub, *Art of Golding*, p. 10.

54. Frank Kermode, 'The Novels of William Golding', *International Literary Annual*, 1961. Reprinted in Nelson, *Golding's Lord of the Flies*, pp. 107–20.

55. Biles, *Talk*, pp. 53–4, 57.

56. Ralph Freedman, 'The New Realism: The Fancy of William Golding', *Perspective*, Summer–Autumn 1958. Reprinted in Nelson, *Golding's Lord of the Flies*, pp. 43–53.

57. '*Lord of the Flies* Goes to College', *The New Republic*, 4 May 1963. Quoted in Bernard F. Dick, *William Golding* (New York: Twayne Publishers, 1967), p. 97.

58. Leighton Hodson, *William Golding* (Edinburgh: Oliver and Boyd, 1969), p. 33.

59. Francis E. Kearns, 'Salinger and Golding: Conflict on the Campus',

America, 26 January 1963. Reprinted in Nelson, *Golding's Lord of the Flies*, pp. 148–55.

60. Luke M. Grande, 'The Appeal of Golding', *Commonweal*, 25 January 1963. Reprinted in Nelson, *Golding's Lord of the Flies*, pp. 156–9.

61. Francis E. Kearns and Luke M. Grande, 'An Exchange of Views', *Commonweal*, 22 February 1963. Reprinted in Nelson, *Golding's Lord of the Flies*, pp. 160–9.

62. Oldsey and Weintraub, *Art of Golding*, pp. 34–5.

63. Whitley, *Golding: Lord of the Flies*, pp. 55–6.

64. Biles, *Talk*, pp. 68–9.

65. Crompton, *Golding's Later Novels*, p. 65.

66. Peter Green, 'The World of William Golding', *Transactions and Proceedings of the Royal Society of Literature*, 1963. Reprinted in Nelson, *Golding's Lord of the Flies*, pp. 170–89.

67. Dick, *William Golding*, p. 100.

68. Crompton, *Golding's Later Novels*, pp. 45–9.

69. Biles, *Talk*, p. 21.

70. *A Moving Target*, pp. 169–70.

71. Biles, *Talk*, p. x.

72. Whitley, *Golding: Lord of the Flies*, pp. 19–21.

73. Oldsey and Weintraub, *Art of Golding*, p. 28 and fn 11.

74. Dick, *William Golding*, preface.

75. Oldsey and Weintraub, *Art of Golding*, p. 17.

76. Howard F. Babb, *The Novels of William Golding* (Columbus, Ohio: Ohio State University Press, 1970), p. 202.

77. Mark Kinkaid-Weekes and Ian Gregor, *William Golding: A Critical Study* (New York: Harcourt, Brace & World, 1968), p. 15.

78. Ibid., p. 243.

79. Hodson, *William Golding*, p. 2.

80. Ian Gregor and Mark Kinkead-Weekes, 'The Strange Case of Mr. Golding and His Critics', *The Twentieth Century*, February 1960. Reprinted in Nelson, *Golding's Lord of the Flies*, pp. 60–70.

81. Crompton, *Golding's Later Novels*, pp. 1–3.

82. Johnston, *Of Earth and Darkness*, pp. 68–9.

83. *A Moving Target*, pp. 164–6.

84. *An Egyptian Journal*, p. 60.

85. Golding, interview with Henry David Rosso, cited in n. 32 above.

86. Ibid.

87. Crompton, *Golding's Later Novels*, p. 187.

88. Apart from speculations about Golding's 'greatness' at the time of the Nobel Prize award, the literary culture produces occasional debates in which the issue of a contemporary's 'greatness' flares as something between simplified publicity and a serious discussion of achievement. One such recent example is the public discussion of whether or not the contemporary Geoffrey Hill is a 'great' poet, treated in several essays in *The London Review of Books* in early 1986 and in the *TLS* of 4 April 1986. The point is that both Golding and Hill are serious, committed, difficult writers attempting to work out different searching statements about contemporary experience. To discuss 'greatness' before time has made or not made the writer a voice that can profoundly

convey his culture to another is both to inflate the perspective of the artist and (more usually) to derogate the achievement by implying a pretentious stance the artist never assumed.

89. Crompton, *Golding's Later Novels*, p. 20.
90. *A Moving Target*, p. 152.
91. Ibid., p. 201.
92. Humphrey Carpenter, *W. H. Auden: A Biography* (London: George Allen and Unwin, 1981), p. 329.

Bibliography

Place of publication is London unless otherwise stated.

GOLDING'S PRINCIPAL WORKS

Poems (Macmillan, 1934).
Lord of the Flies (Faber and Faber, 1954).
The Inheritors (Faber and Faber, 1955).
Pincher Martin (Faber and Faber, 1956).
The Brass Butterfly (Faber and Faber, 1958).
Free Fall (Faber and Faber, 1959).
The Spire (Faber and Faber, 1964).
The Hot Gates and Other Occasional Pieces (Faber and Faber, 1965).
The Pyramid (Faber and Faber, 1967).
The Scorpion God: Three Short Novels (Faber and Faber, 1971).
Darkness Visible (Faber and Faber, 1979).
Rites of Passage (Faber and Faber, 1980).
A Moving Target (Faber and Faber, 1982).
The Paper Men (Faber and Faber, 1984).
An Egyptian Journal (London and Boston: Faber and Faber, 1985).

SELECTED SECONDARY SOURCES

Babb, Howard S., *The Novels of William Golding* (Colombus, Ohio: Ohio State University Press, 1970).
Biles, Jack I., *Talk: Conversation with William Golding* (New York: Harcourt Brace Jovanovich, 1970).
Crompton, Don, *A View from the Spire: William Golding's Later Novels*, edited and completed by Julia Briggs (Oxford: Blackwell, 1985).
Dick, Bernard F., *William Golding* (New York: Twayne Publishers, 1967).
Hodson, Leighton, *William Golding* (Edinburgh: Oliver and Boyd, 1969).
Hynes, Samuel, *William Golding*, Columbia Essays on Modern Writers, No. 2 (New York and London: Columbia University Press, 1964).
Johnston, Arnold, *Of Earth and Darkness: The Novels of William Golding* (Columbia, Mo. and London: University of Missouri Press, 1980).

Kermode, Frank and Golding, William, 'The Meaning of it All', broadcast on the BBC Third Programme, 28 August 1959. Transcript published in *Books and Bookmen* (October 1959).

Kinkead-Weakes, Mark, and Gregor, Ian, *William Golding: A Critical Study* (New York: Harcourt, Brace & World, Inc., 1967).

Nelson, William (ed.), *William Golding's Lord of the Flies: A Source Book* (New York: Odyssey Press, 1963).

Oldsey, Bernard S. and Weintraub, Stanley, *The Art of William Golding*, (Bloomington, Indiana and London: Indiana University Press, 1965).

Page, Norman (ed.), *William Golding: Novels 1954–67: A Selection of Literary Criticism*, Casebook Series (Macmillan, 1985).

Tiger, Virginina, *William Golding: The Dark Fields of Discovery* (Calder and Boyars, 1974).

Whitley, John S., *Golding: Lord of the Flies*, Studies in English Literature, No. 42 (Edward Arnold, 1970).

Index